QUILTS
An American Heritage

TERRI ZEGART

With a Foreword by
SHELLY ZEGART

SMITHMARK

ACKNOWLEDGMENTS

I am deeply grateful to the following people for their invaluable assistance, time, support, and energy in helping me bring this book to fruition: Shelly Zegart, Kenny Zegart, Amy Zegart, Stacy Roof, Dorothy West, Velma Vaughan and David Roth. My thanks also to Joel Kopp of America Hurrah Antiques, New York City, and to The Kentucky Quilt Project Inc., Louisville, Kentucky, for allowing us to include their photographs.

This edition published in 1994 by SMITHMARK Publishers Inc., 16 East 32nd Street, New York, NY 10016

SMITHMARK books are available for bulk purchase for sales promotion and premium use. For details write or call the manager of special sales, SMITHMARK Publishers Inc., 16 East 32nd Street, New York, NY 10016; (212) 532-6600.

This book was designed and produced by
Todtri Productions Limited
P.O. Box 20058
New York, NY 10023-1482

Printed and Bound in Singapore

10 9 8 7 6 5 4 3 2 1

Library of Congress Catalog Card Number 94-065425

ISBN 0-8317-0420-9

Author: Terri Zegart

Producer: Robert M. Tod
Book Designer: Mark Weinberg
Production Coordinator: Heather Weigel
Photo Editor: Edward Douglas
Editors: Mary Forsell, Joanna Wissinger, & Don Kennison
Design Associates: Josh Cheuse, Jackie Skroczky, & Adam Yellin

Preceding page:
Nature is always an inspiration to the quilt maker, and the star is one of the most frequent themes in pieced quilts. In this quilt the quilt maker pieced tulips into the design along with the stars.

Right:
Log Cabin quilts symbolized the pioneer spirits of independence and self-reliance. The addition of the appliquéd red and green Princess Feather center and the star corner blocks adds to the complexity and sophistication of the design.

Contents

*This version of the Double Wedding Ring is often called Pickle Dish or
Indian Wedding Ring by different makers. The Double Wedding Ring
was one of the three most popular patterns in the 1920s and 1930s.*

Foreword

Antique quilts are both historical documents and personal diaries. Historically, they tell not only of personal triumphs, milestones, and tragedies, but also of cultural, ethnic, and social influences—of migration patterns, weather patterns, and changes in technology. The intent of this book is to examine the regional differences of quilt design and quilt making in the United States. But first, we must understand how the lives and times of quilters influenced the development of the art.

Contrary to the popular American notion that quilting is indigenous to the United States, the first colonists brought with them strong quilting traditions. And while the origins of quilting remain a mystery, it is known that quilting has been practiced in many different parts of the world from the earliest of times. For example, the carved figure of a pharaoh of the Egyptian First Dynasty, dating back to 3400 BC, was found wearing a quilted garment, while the earliest known bed quilt is a Sicilian quilt dating back to the fourteenth century. There was also a flurry of quilt making in India in the early sixteenth century—substantiated by the records of merchants who traveled there. And it is known that Great Britain had a long tradition of quilt making, as did many other European countries.

Along with quilting traditions, the settlers brought their cultural values and religious beliefs, reflected in the colors, patterns, styles, techniques, and fabrics of quilts made in the New World. The impact of economics and geography as well as mandates imposed by the mother countries resulted in a wide disparity of customs and styles from group to group and area to area. Customs of dress influenced the materials and colors used in the making of quilts. One example is the Amish, whose religious faith governed their lifestyle. Because the use of fancy printed fabrics and bright, ostentatious colors was forbidden, Amish quilts were (and still are) distinguished by their muted solid colors and simple geometric patterns.

While the early settlers retained their European traditions and customs, they were also forced, out of necessity, to modify and adapt to life in the New World. For instance, the settlers had to build their own shelters. One such shelter was the log cabin, which came to symbolize the independent, self-reliant spirit of the pioneers and the importance of home and community. Therefore, it is not surprising that Log Cabin quilts were made all over the United States. In fact, many of the early quilt pattern names reflected various aspects of a pioneer's life. Straight Furrow referred to plowed fields while Barn Raising referred to the communal effort necessary to build a barn for a family. Weather, in various areas of the country, dictated the type or thickness of the fabric and colors used, and was also reflected in quilt pattern names, such as Streak of Lightning.

War, politics, economic depression, agricultural fairs, and quilting bees all affected the development of quilt making in the United States. The woman's role in the early years of the country centered around the household with daily chores that often required hard physical labor. Quilting and quilting bees offered a temporary respite from the everyday grind. They provided a chance to socialize as well as an outlet for self-expression. State and county Agricultural Fairs, established in 1841, offered women a chance to make quilts on a competitive basis. These fairs exposed women to new colors, fabrics, and patterns that spread across the country. Later, during the Civil War, women organized various Soldier's Aid Societies and collected food, clothing, quilts, and bedding to distribute to injured soldiers. More than 250,000 quilts were said to have been collected and given to soldiers of the North. In 1876, the United States celebrated its centennial in Philadelphia with gala events and exhibits. What took place in Philadelphia spurred the emergence of the American Arts and Crafts movement.

The movement, strongly influenced by the Japanese exhibit seen at the Centennial, emphasized the artistry of quilt making but frowned upon traditional patchwork. In response, the Crazy quilt, which featured many Japanese motifs, was born. The Crazy quilt (often called the first "art quilt"), unlike most other quilts of the period, was rarely intended for use as a bed cover. Rather, it was a work of art that reflected the moral pressure on women of the late Victorian era to create a

The Baskets pattern can be expanded in numerous ways. This quilt combines Baskets with Nine Patches, Triangles, Flying Geese, and multiple borders.

beautiful home.

Events that affected the entire country also affected quilt making in dramatic ways. For example, the assassination of President McKinley on September 6, 1901, triggered a flurry of commemorative quilts memorializing the beloved leader. The Great Depression of the 1930s forced families to be thrifty and self-reliant; many quilts of that period were made out of recycled grain and feed bags.

Toward the end of the nineteenth century, more people were moving into newly developed cities and towns. New experiences, social contacts, and employment opportunities in these metropolitan areas changed their lives in fundamental ways. For example, previously, the occasional quilting bee had been the most important social event of the year for many women, but in towns and cities there were various church groups and other organizations that gathered more frequently. Additionally, there were quilting bees for missionary societies and other worthy causes that often met on a weekly basis.

Women's roles in society were changing as it became more acceptable for women to meet outside of their homes. Many were able to assume leadership roles quickly. With a decrease in the necessity for hard, physical domestic labor, women had more time to devote to social and political causes. Quilt making became a channel for women to express their opinions and influence or promote change in society.

The Hexagon is one of the oldest of the pieced patterns. As early as 1835, Godey's Ladies Book gave instructions for the making of a Hexagon or Honeycomb pieced quilt.

The technological changes that occurred in the United States during this period— the advent of the cotton gin in 1793, the sewing machine in the 1840s, and the development and growth of the textile industry—also affected quilting. Advances in transportation and communication joined people together from all over the country. People were able to move more easily around the continent taking their quilts and quilt patterns with them wherever they went. Various periodicals kept homemakers up to date with the latest styles. Of particular importance to quilt making at the time was women's ability to order patterns, fabric, and supplies by mail, allowing them increased opportunities to express themselves in new ways.

There have been several periods of intense interest in quilt making throughout the twentieth century. We are currently in the midst of a worldwide quilt revival which began in the early 1970s. Over nine million people are either quilting or interested in some part of the quilt phenomenon. An explosion of publications, exhibitions, festivals, shops, classes, and contests has developed to meet this interest. Today's quilt artists stretch the boundaries of their medium to create works of art—comparable in quality and creativity to paintings and other works of art displayed in museums around the world.

—Shelly Zegart

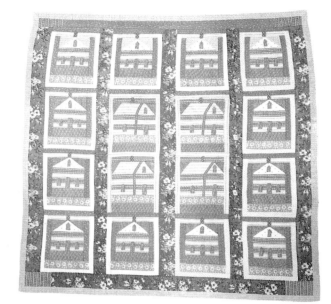

Most Schoolhouse quilts show one architectural elevation. This quilt is unique because it shows both front and side. The Schoolhouse pattern first appeared late in the nineteenth century.

This quilt maker merged two late Victorian quilting styles. Crazy quilts were the first "art quilts" and were used as decorative elements within the Victorian home.

Although it recalls a Western sunset, this Blazing Star could also have been made in New York or Pennsylvania. Its precision of design, execution, and color makes it an outstanding example of a quilt from the 1840s.

*Many patterns, both pieced and
appliquéd, abound in this glorious quilt.*

*As early as Revolutionary times, the art of cutting paper
to create ornamental designs was popular in America.*

The maker of this quilt, Mary Kreyenhangen, grew up in Cincinnati, Ohio. Her mother, Marie, owned a dry goods store on McMillan Street. During World War II, her mother used fabrics from her store to depict the town on a quilt. Different prints represent the window displays of various stores—shoes for the shoe store, vegetables for the grocery store. Mary, an artist, portrayed herself as a young girl painting at her easel.

The making of Bible quilts may be unique to Southern black women. These quilts show the strength of the oral tradition within the African-American experience. Two Bible scenes, the Crucifixion and Adam and Eve, are shown in this quilt.

Introduction

*T*his book examines regional differences in quilts and quilt making from the nineteenth through the early twentieth centuries, while also examining the influences of culture, ethnicity, religion, economics, war, politics, social events, and technology on each and every quilt. Only a few states and their patterns are discussed in each of the four chapters. Each chapter is laid out similarly, contingent on the extent of the information available: a brief historical background of the region; migration within and across state lines; rural versus urban quilt making; colors, types of fabrics, and patterns particular to the state or region.

The research for this book was based on state and regional

The women of Liberia made this quilt to honor the Reverend James Edward East, executive secretary of the Foreign Mission Board of the National Baptist Convention of the United States of America in 1822. Inscribed on the quilt are the words "Gift to Reverend James E. East."

Star quilts come in countless shapes and sizes. They are often sewn on a dark background so that the stars appear to be sparkling in the night sky.

documentation projects, the oldest being The Kentucky Quilt Project, begun in 1981. Its catalogue, Kentucky Quilts: 1800-1900, is currently in its third printing. Its exhibition, "Kentucky Quilts: 1800-1900," traveled with the Smithsonian Institution Traveling Exhibition Service to fifteen museums in the United States and Ireland over a two-year period from 1983 to 1985. Since this landmark project, as the directors of the project note on the back cover of the 1992 edition of the catalogue, groups in forty-eight states have undertaken quilt surveys inspired by the methods of The Kentucky Quilt Project. It is estimated that as of early 1992, over 141,000 quilts had been documented, twenty-two publications produced, and over 650 Quilt Days held nationwide. The documentation projects are said to be the largest grassroots movement

in the decorative arts in the last half of the twentieth century, the only other being the American Index of Design, created during the Depression.

Keep in mind that the documentation projects differed widely. They did not all use the same criteria, have the same type of funding, the same type or amount of staff support, hold an equal number of quilt documentation days, or even use the same process for documentation. Each project achieved what it could within its own parameters. The resulting publications do not all include similar information. Some discuss the history of the state and place quilt making in that context, while others simply illustrate the quilts, with their stories forming the main body of text.

Analysis of this material has just begun. There has not yet been any formal attempt to organize the data across project boundaries, although interdisciplinary examination of the data has officially begun with the work of the Lancaster Quilt Harvest in Pennsylvania in 1993. The directors of many of the quilt documentation projects met for the first time at Franklin and Marshall College, Pennsylvania,

Postage Stamp quilts are pieced from hundreds of scrap pieces of fabric, usually less than an inch in size or about the size of a postage stamp. They were usually made up of as many colors and prints as possible in order to show off the quilt maker's skill. Piecing the small pieces into strips and then joining the strips so that seams match and the entire piece remains smooth and unpuckered was a difficult task.

The original patterns for many of the designs of flowers, spiders, and butterflies used on Crazy quilts can be found in women's magazines, department store brochures, and books on handwork of the 1880s.

in June 1993 to discuss the need to improve access to the data and to consider developing a standardized format to facilitate retrieval of quilt data.

The academic study of quilts and quilt making is in its infancy. New research by scholars in a variety of disciplines is moving the field forward every day. This book begins to look closely at regional differences in quilts—something that has not previously been done. It is a brief initial study of nineteenth and early twentieth century quilts that I hope will lead to further exploration of the regional differences in quilts and their makers and will in time also include the quilts and quilt makers of the late twentieth century.

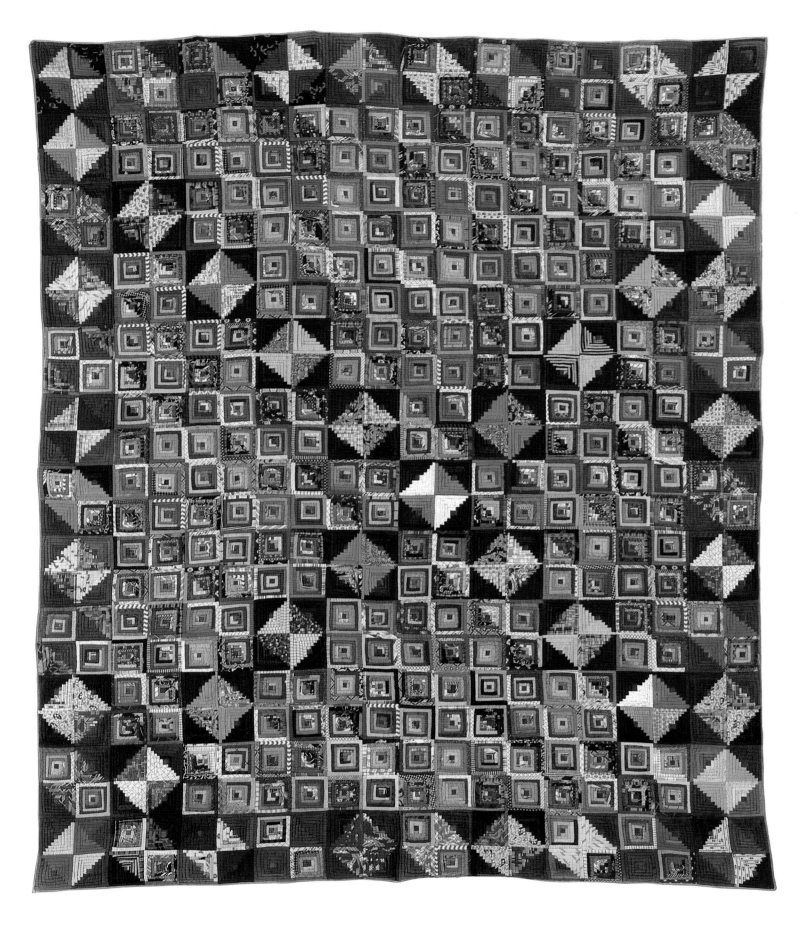

The name Log Cabin comes from the way in which the design is created.
One piece of fabric is layered on top of another, just as a cabin is built by layering one
log on another. The square at the center of each block is called the chimney.

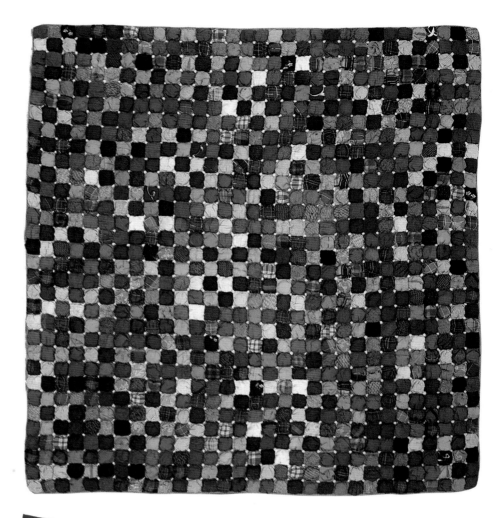

This is an example of the late Victorian craze for novelty textiles, which included parlor throws, Cigar Band quilts, and Crazy quilts.

Flowers were not only used in quilts as representational forms, but also in an abstract geometric form.

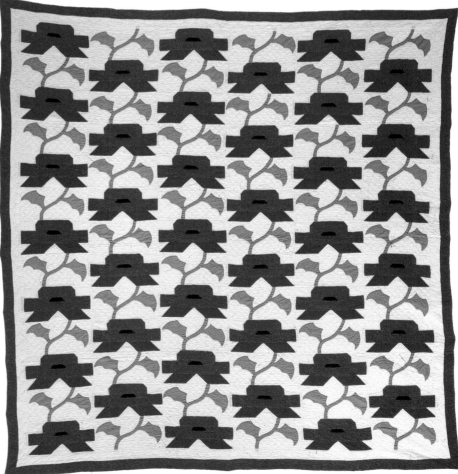

The bandanna used as the center medallion was a symbol of the Republican presidential campaign of 1880. The standard bearers, James A. Garfield of Ohio and Chester A. Arthur of New York, won the election. Garfield was the twentieth president, Arthur the twenty-first (after Garfield was assassinated in office).

"You have to have a little artist about you," a quilter once said, explaining the impulse that keeps quilters piecing and quilting by hand in an era of widely available, inexpensive, machine-made blankets and comforters.

*This Medallion quilt in 1870s fabrics illustrates the
inspiration of the quilt maker. Both the Star and the
Flying Geese patterns are frequently used themes.*

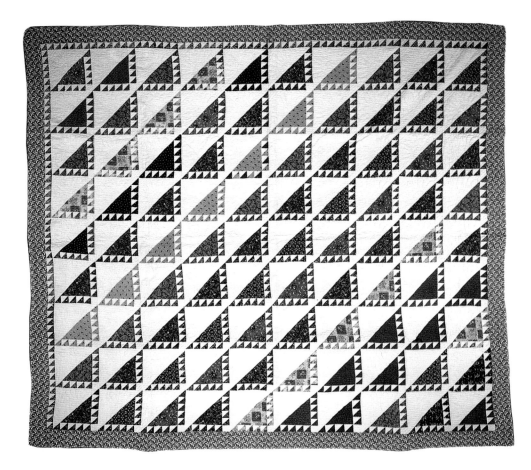

Quilt makers of the past created designs based on geometric shapes—squares, rectangles, triangles— when they had the luxury of using a whole piece of cloth. Triangles have always been popular because of their simplicity and versatility.

CHAPTER ONE:

The Northeast

New York State had a great deal to offer early settlers, many of whom were English or Dutch. Aside from boasting many natural resources, the state's location on the Atlantic coast provided numerous harbors as well as access to inland water routes. Not surprisingly, New York soon became a commercial center for textile manufacturing.

Prior to 1750, in order to protect itself from competition, the Dutch West India Company had prohibited the manufacture of textiles in the colonies. The British Navigation Act of 1651 and the 1699 Wool Act further curtailed textile production in the colonies. Such restrictions eventually created shortages, as the linens and clothing colonists had brought with them began to wear out. Moreover, the restrictions encouraged illicit home production and smuggling.

Though flax was also an important fiber in the early colonial days, the Northeast's cold winters demanded the warmth of wool. To color these fabrics, colonists took advantage of the abundant vegetation in the region to make vegetable and bark dyes. The colors of many quilts in the North tended to be darker than those in the South because of the differences in climates. In their research on Southern quilts, Bets Ramsey and Gail Andrews Trechsel note that light colors, especially white backgrounds, were preferred in the South. In the North, where winters were long and summers were chilly at night, quilts generally displayed richer, deeper colors to absorb the sunlight, and provide actual warmth as well as a feeling of warmth.

Until the end of the Revolutionary War, there were surges of textile imports. However, after the war, colonists recognized that home production was essential to maintain their industrial and political independence. So they set to work to improve not only the size and capabilities of textile mills in this country, but also the quality of the materials produced.

The first domestic textile mills were established in New England. These mills produced an abundance of fine fabrics; thus quilts in the Northeast were typically made from scraps of fine new material left over from the making of clothes and various other projects. Northern mills also supplied fine percales for its quilt makers to use for quilt backs, as well as fine thread.

The use of scraps of old clothing created a quilt that today would be considered a work of art.

By 1800, small carding mills could be found in virtually every township in New York that had access to water power. Soon after, many New Englanders began moving west in search of better farmland, bringing with them the technology needed to establish and operate cotton mills. By 1810 New York had twenty-six cotton mills.

In their book *New York Beauties: Quilts from the Empire State*, Jacqueline Atkins and Phyllis Tepper point out that during the first quarter of the nineteenth century in the rural areas of states like New York, a combination of factory and domestic manufacture continued to exist, especially in the western section of the state, where access to supplies and neccessities was limited. However, by the time the Erie Canal opened in 1825, most of the cities and towns in western New York played at least a minor role in the textile industry.

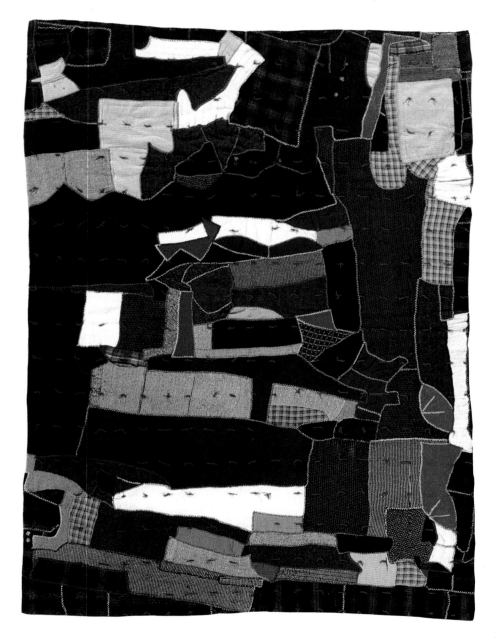

In those areas of the Northeast where the textile industry had not developed and where there were few places to purchase household items of any kind, colonists depended on peddlers who traveled on foot, on horseback, or by wagon to bring them the household items they needed, including those needed for sewing. In many cases when a peddler did not have a specific item with him, he would request it from his supplier and bring it with him on his next visit. With respect to fabrics, the peddler sometimes dictated, by default, the colors and patterns a quilter used because his supplier simply could not fulfill the customer's request.

Peddlers were also often a source for quilt designs. In their travels, they sometimes passed on information about patterns or templates for a popular pattern in exchange for a place to sleep or a good meal. Although the peddler had virtually disappeared by the last

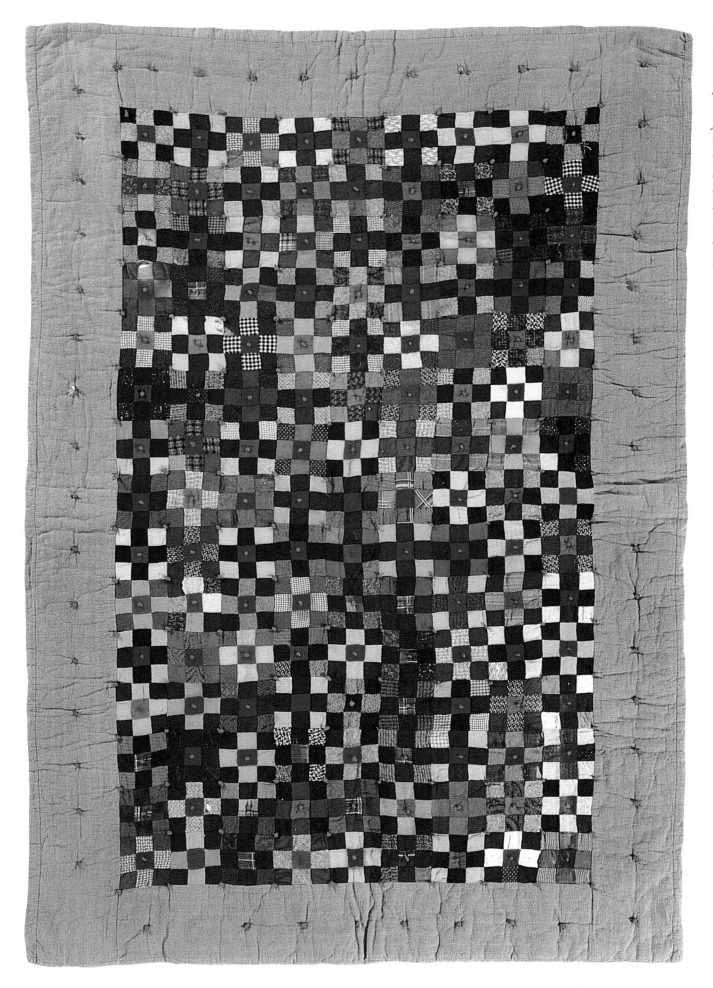

Quilts like this one are characterized by simple patchwork patterns, coarse fabrics, batting of thick cotton or wool, and little or no quilting— many are tied with yarn rather than stitched. Most were made after the Civil War.

Following page: Dating from the late Victorian era, this novelty quilt was sewn from silk cigar bands printed with brand names.

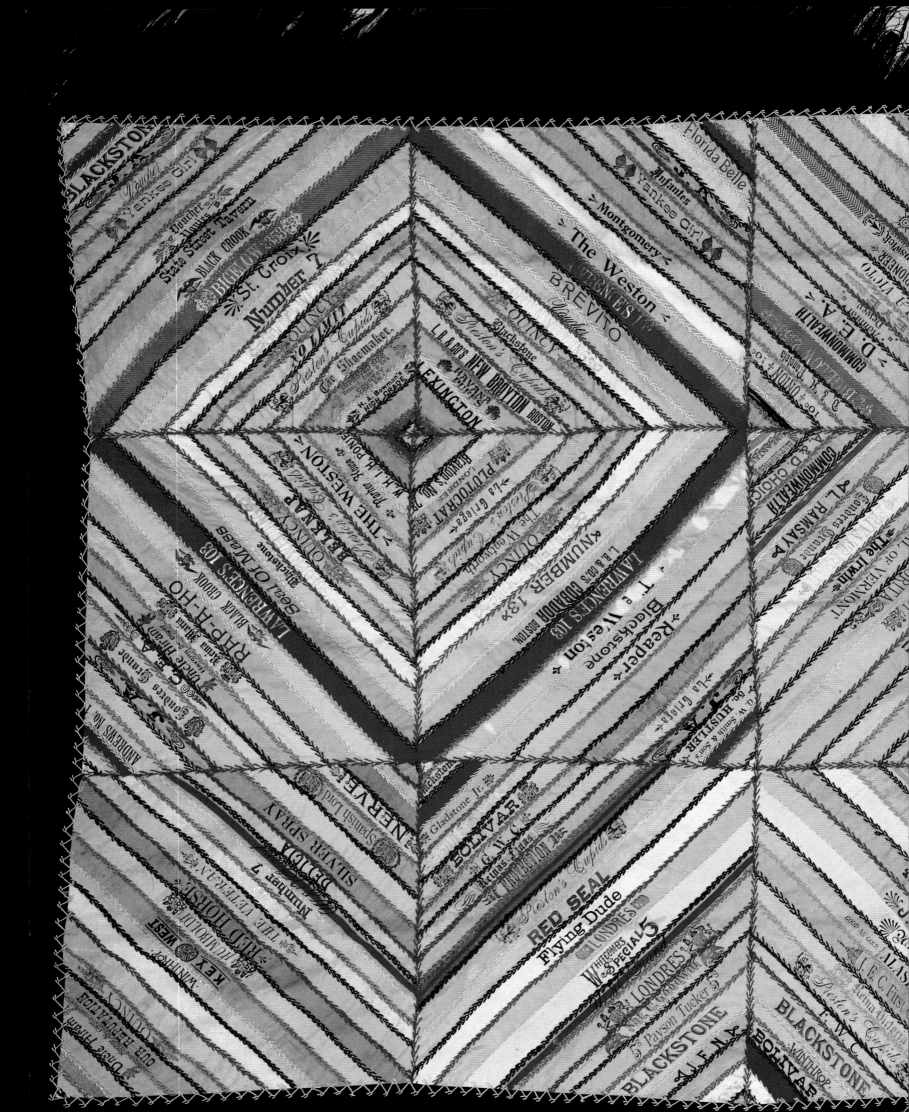

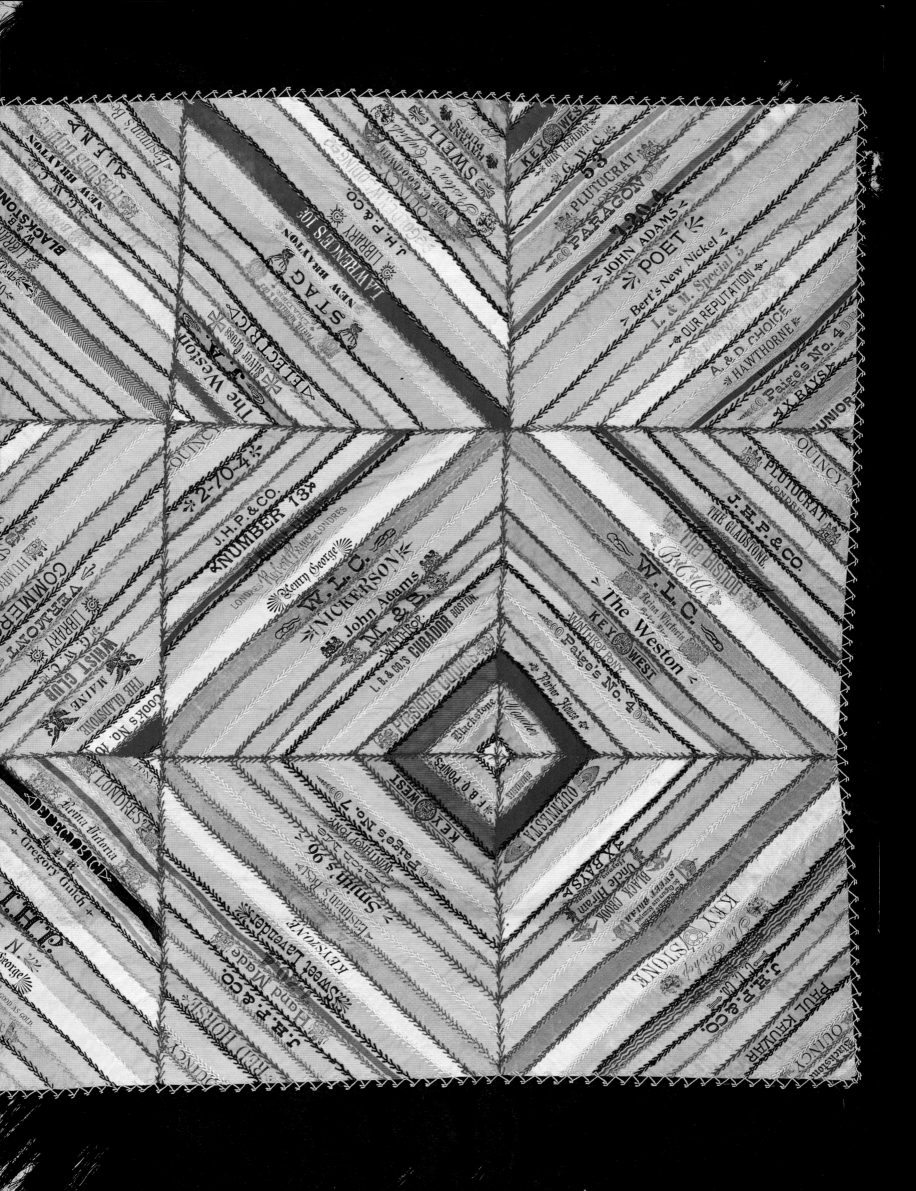

quarter of the nineteenth century, he continued to be an important supplier of household items in more rural parts of the Northeast up until the era of the automobile.

NEW YORK

By 1840 textile manufacturing was one of the largest industries in the state of New York, and New York City had established itself as the hub of the country's textile market. By the time of the Civil War, Americans were buying most of their fabrics in New York or through New York companies. However, textile manufacturing in the state began to decline significantly during the latter part of the nineteenth century. By the 1920s, in fact, the base of textile production had shifted to the South, leaving few mills or

Squares of block-printed textiles, c. 1825, have been put together in a Medallion format. This design originally came to the United States from England.

The Irish Chain was a pattern of great popularity. It appeared in many color variations and is a derivation of the One Patch.

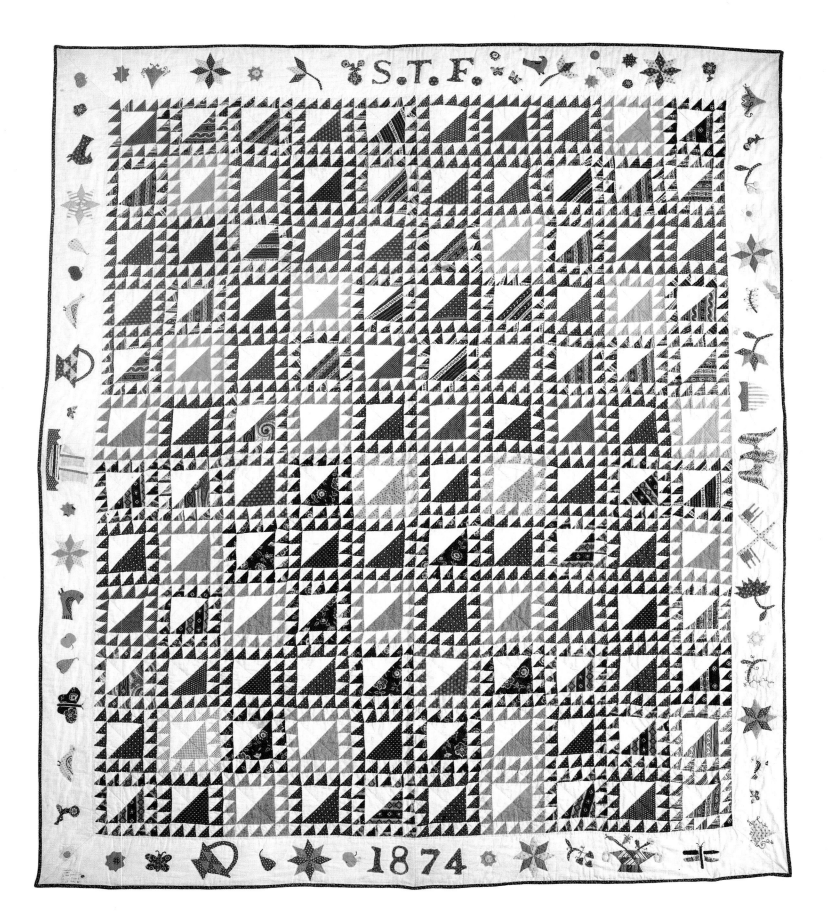

Patterns with such intriguing names as *Flying Geese* and *Birds in the Air* are favorites based on the use of triangular patches, as are stylized tulips. These patterns suggest the movement of birds in flight. Signed and dated quilts are uncommon. The maker of this quilt also appliquéd ships, shields, flags, and other patriotic motifs around the border.

The name of this quilt, Delectable Mountains, is taken from
a passage in John Bunyan's Pilgrim's Progress, published in 1678.
This quilt displays many of the wonderful fabrics of the era.

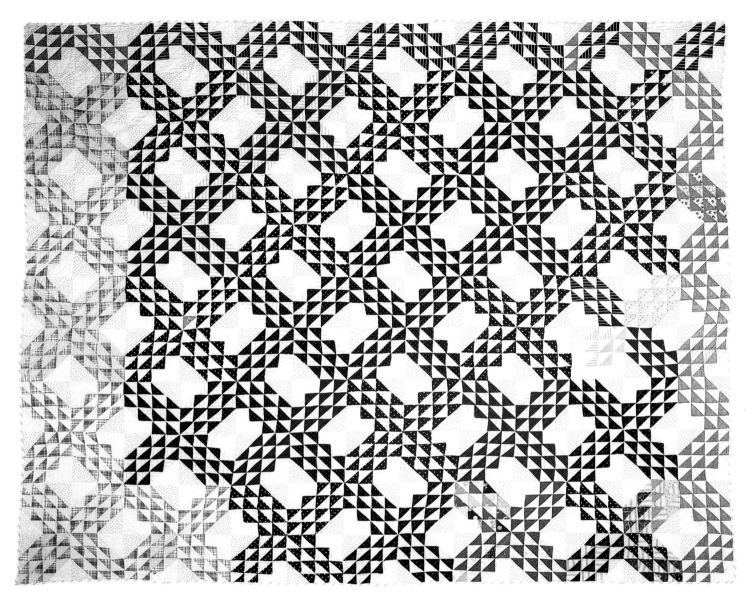

The Ocean Waves quilt consists of a block design of pieced triangles, an abstract depiction of the ocean's movement. It dates from the 1870s.

Cold weather made wool quilts necessary for bed coverings. The Variable Star appeared in the first half of the eighteenth century, making it one of the earliest known patterns.

Women all over the world have made wool quilts and comforters from used clothing. These quilts have a number of regional names: "haps" in England and in parts of Pennsylvania and "suggans" in Texas. In Australia they are known as "waggas."

*Blue and white has always been a popular color
combination for quilts. This design was most likely
a prized possession of the family that owned it.*

print operations in business.

The fabrics seen in the quilts reviewed for the New York State Quilt Project, which began in 1988, reflected the popular tastes, fashions, and colors of the time (as well as their availability). However, as Jacqueline Atkins and Phyllis Tepper have found, no quilt pattern or design typifies the state. Further, they found that, "no strong regional styles could really be identified among the more than 6,000 quilts reviewed during the Project."[1] The patterns listed here are those determined by the New York State Quilt Project to be, by virtue of the number of quilts documented, the favorite patterns of New York State quilt makers. They include: Stars (single and multiple), Log Cabin, Basket, Grandmother's Flower Garden, Chimney Sweep, Irish Chain, and Nine Patch. While these were the predominant patterns documented, they are but a few of the many patterns registered during the New York State Quilt Project—most of them familiar, but some of them unknown, whose origins may never be determined.

There are many variations on the Basket pattern, including fruit baskets, flower baskets, and cactus baskets. Baskets were a popular pattern because the quilter could vary the contents of the basket or its piecing. This example is initialed and dated 1853.

The Chimney Sweep pattern, also called an Album Patch, was the perfect choice for applying signatures.

Flying Geese quilts have always been a popular design. Example of textiles of the era can be found in pieced quilts made throughout the country.

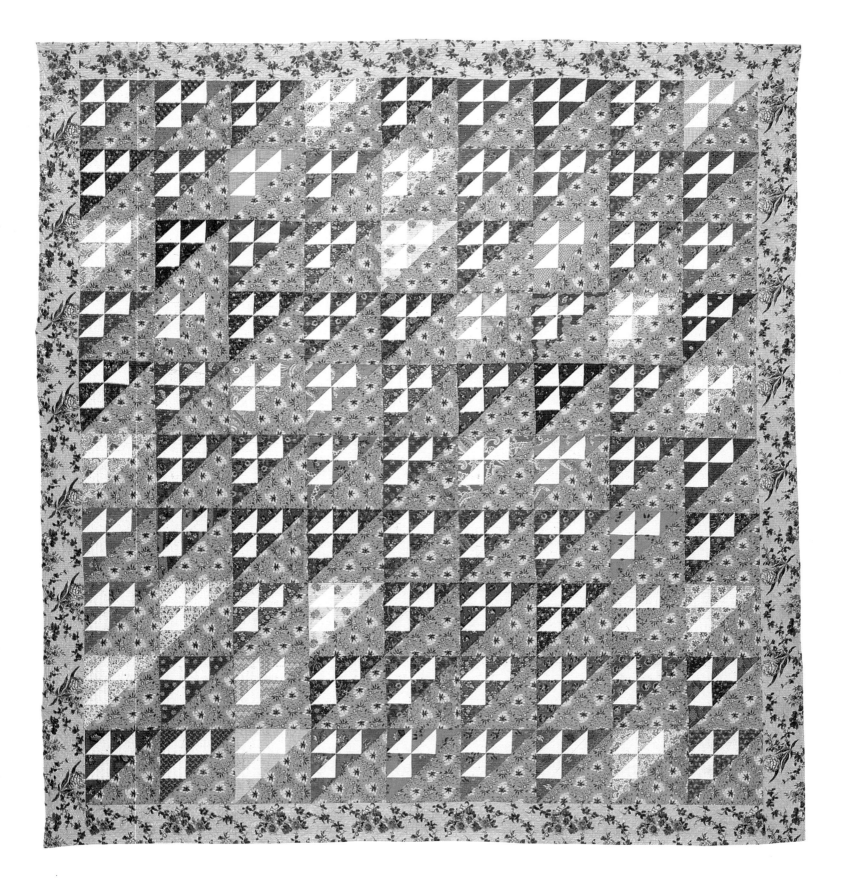

*This pattern, Birds in the Air, is another
example of a design abstracted from nature.*

Diamond in the Square is one of the oldest and simplest Amish patterns. With this example it is difficult to decide which is more outstanding—the bold pattern or the sophisticated quilting.

PENNSYLVANIA

In the heart of Pennsylvania, people of English, Scotch-Irish, and German descent lived side by side. Stars in all sorts of variations, particularly the Star of Bethlehem, were favorite images. Only the beginner's Nine Patch outnumbered star patterns here. Most women pieced and appliquéd their work in cottons. In fact, appliqué patterns were more popular than patchwork in the mid-nineteenth century. This trend continued for close to fifty years. Color and fabric combinations of appliquéd quilts of the time generally consisted of red and green calicos stitched onto a white top with occasional accents of yellow, orange, or pink. Pink and green were the predominant colors in pieced quilts. Studies of quilting in other areas in Pennsylvania have also yielded similar results, with the exception of the Amish. Jeannette Lasansky published a series of papers through her Oral Traditions Project in 1985 that discussed this research.

The quilts of the Amish are an expression of their way of life, which dictates the use of color and design and holds simplicity and symbolism in the highest regard. The Amish value objects of high quality and derive pleasure from creating useful and beautiful pieces, but this pleasure must be balanced against their all-encompassing religious beliefs. The tensions that arise out of this are reflected in Amish quilts.

Contrary to popular belief, most of the Amish quilts known and documented to date were made

This quilt was made by the Pennsylvania Amish. The Bars pattern could have been inspired by plowed fields or horizontal slats on wood fences. Amish quilts avoid the realistic reproduction of an object.

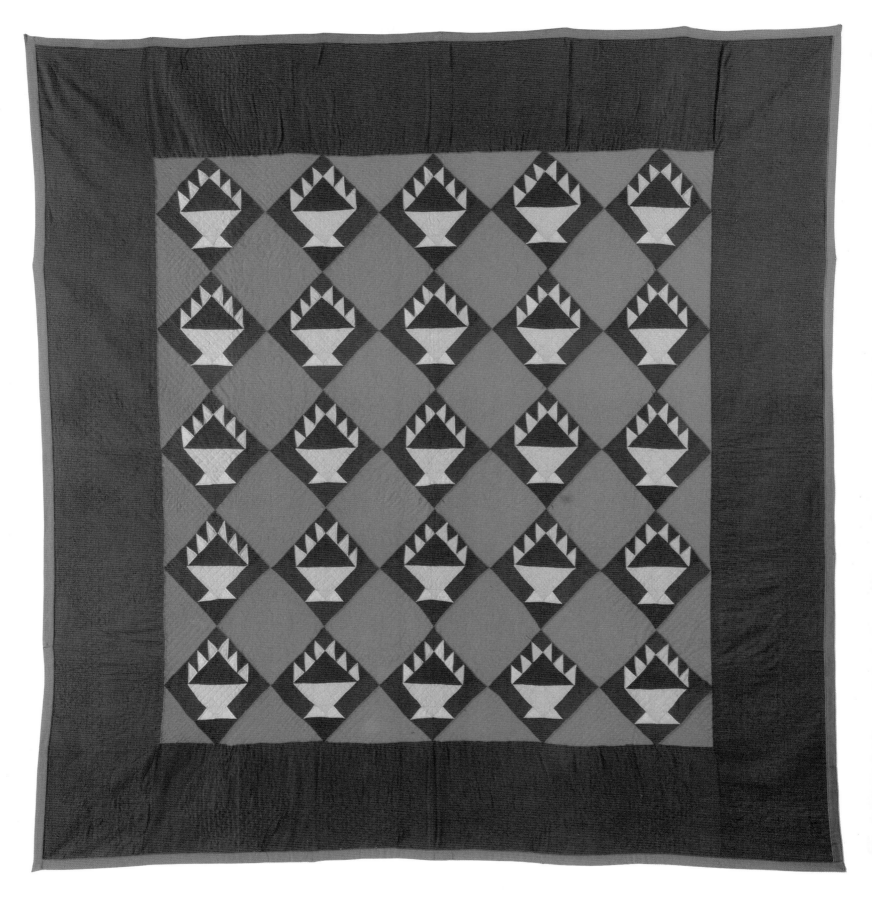

*Amish Basket quilts were mostly made in the Midwest. Residents of
Lancaster County, Pennsylvania (the source of this quilt), are descendants
of eighteenth-century immigrants who came to Pennsylvania.*

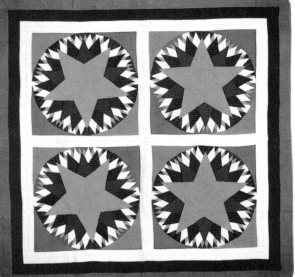

The names of patterns reveal the imagination of the quilt maker, as in this example, Stars in the Window.

The Double Nine Patch uses five nine-patch squares, combined with four solid squares of equal size, to form the whole. The numerous possibilities of color and pattern make this seemingly simple design highly intriguing.

between the 1880s and the 1960s, with the majority being made in the twentieth century. When the Amish did begin to make quilts, they seem to have deliberately used the most unfashionable and simple patterns.

The oldest continuously occupied Amish community in the United States is in Lancaster County, Pennsylvania. The Amish of this community, compared with their non-Amish neighbors, were rather late in embarking on quilt making. Once they did, however, their quilt making was thoroughly permeated with their traditions. As a result, Lancaster Amish quilts are distinctively different from quilts made by other Amish communities in the United States. While the color, fabric, and needlework of Lancaster Amish quilts have considerably changed over the years, the patterns of these quilts today are essentially the same as those of the late nineteenth century and early twentieth century.

Joseph's Coat was a favorite pattern among the Mennonites in eastern Pennsylvania.

The most popular of these designs include Baskets, Diamond in the Square, Sunshine and Shadow, and Bars. The Diamond in the Square pattern is unique in that it is rarely found outside of Lancaster County. When this pattern is found elsewhere, it generally means that someone with ties to Lancaster made the quilt. The same is true with certain colors that can be attributed to Lancaster County, such as deep shades of brown, rust, wine, olive, and forest green. If bright colors were used at all they were juxtaposed with the more neutral colors.

Particularly among Amish communities of Ohio and Indiana, differences in color and quilt designs reflect migration patterns and other factors that will be further disscussed. Most of the research on this subject has been presented by Eve Wheatcroft Granick in *The Amish Quilt*.

The woman who made this quilt did her own variation of the Joseph's Coat pattern. She must have been proud of it because she placed her initials and the date in the center block.

The birds and flowers represented here could have been inspired by other examples of nineteenth-century Pennsylvania folk art.

Myriad plant, bird, and flower images appear in quilt patterns. Undoubtedly, this quilt depicts birds whirling in the sunlight.

Many quilters used bright colors and traditional German symbols in their quilts. The combinations are dazzling.

Susie Gorrel Harvey and her sister made this quilt in Baltimore, Maryland, around 1854. It was passed along to Susie's daughter, Maude Harvey Moeller, who later remarried. Susie then gave the quilt to another relative, Dorothy Jo, who gave it to her daughter, Dorothy Harsher.

BALTIMORE, MARYLAND

When one thinks of Baltimore and quilting, Baltimore Album quilts immediately come to mind. The making of Album quilts in general was tremendously popular in the middle decades of the nineteenth century, but it is the Baltimore Album quilts that are distinguished by their beauty, unique attributes, and sheer numbers. They are highly prized by quilt collectors.

Curiously, no one knows much about who made the Baltimore Album quilts or even why they were made. It is said that some quilts and individual blocks were made by a woman, Mary Evans, and then sold commercially. There is, however, not much

evidence to support this theory. It is known that many of these quilts and their blocks were made by groups of women within specific churches in Baltimore. Whatever the case may be, it is clear that the making of Baltimore Album quilts was more than just a hobby for the quilt makers. These quilts have always had a great deal of emotion and meaning attached to them.

As their name suggests, Album quilts, like photo albums or scrap books, revolve around a central theme, such as friendship and marriage. They are a collection of blocks put together to tell a story—a story that conjures memories of the Album's maker and serves as a keepsake for the receiver of the special quilt.

Both technology and demography affected the development and creation of Baltimore Album

Some Album quilts are believed to be the work of one woman and not a group. You can identify the work of one person by the uniformity of the stitching.

quilts. New dyes and inks as well as the rich fabrics available in Baltimore no doubt stimulated the making of these designs. Moreover, since New York and Baltimore were the two largest seaports in the nation at the time, there was a certain level of sophistication found in both regions that no doubt filtered down into quilt making.

How can one explain the Album phenomenon? Moreover, what does cultural history tell us? Elly Sienkiewicz says, in *Baltimore Beauties and Beyond: Volume Two*, that one must begin with a look at Victorian America, which placed a high value on human attachments and connections. Narrowing her focus to Baltimore, she states that "Baltimore Albums are threaded both literally and symbolically with the concepts of civic caring, patriotism, and personal loyalty, benevolence and 'Christian virtues,' and friendship,"[2] explaining the desire to make, give, and receive these quilts as follows: "Migrations to western territories kept America on the move. In a bustling seaport such as Baltimore, fare-thee-wells must have been commonplace. The desire to make remembrances for friends and family moving away was surely one reason for Album Quilts in the middle decades of the nineteenth century. These quilts would have covered attachments, stitched them finely in, and thus served as comforts to both those leaving and to those being left behind."[3]

Album quilts were often composed of elaborate blocks designed and quilted by a group of women. During the mid-nineteenth century, all types of Album quilts were fashionable.

finely in, and thus served as comforts to both those leaving and to those being left behind." [3]

Baltimore Album quilts give the sense that something important had happened, was happening, or was expected to happen. The mid-nineteenth century was an extremely social era in the United States. All sorts of causes flourished during this period, including the women's rights movement. It was the Age of Progress, of Western Expansion, of the City Beautiful movement, and a time when the belief in Manifest Destiny of the United States was firmly established. Railroads had begun to connect many cities and new inventions permitted more leisure time. At the same time, it was a troubled and unsettled period. A war occurred over the annexation of Texas, while the threat of war loomed over the question of whether or not the Union should admit new territories as slave states or free ones.

Yet throughout the turmoil of the period, beautiful quilts were made, quilts that set a standard of excellence for future quilt makers.

Album quilts enjoyed a great vogue near Baltimore during the 1840s and 1850s. Enterprising seamstresses often supplied both quilt blocks and patterns for sale.

The Rose is the most frequently found floral
pattern. Many of the Rose patterns depicted all aspects
of the plant, including buds, leaves, flowers, and stems.

This Shoo-fly pattern is active and dizzy, almost an Op Art image.

CHAPTER TWO:

The South, Southeast, and Southwest

Those who settled on land south of the Potomac River were primarily of English, French, German, Swiss, African, and Scotch-Irish origin. The economy played a major role in the domestic practices in the South and distinguished it from other regions of the country. Agricultural production predominated in the South, while manufacturing flourished in other parts of the country first. Southern coastal newcomers bought large areas of land and raised lucrative crops. It wasn't long before an affluent upper class established itself. Since farmers had easy access to seaports, they were able to obtain imports for

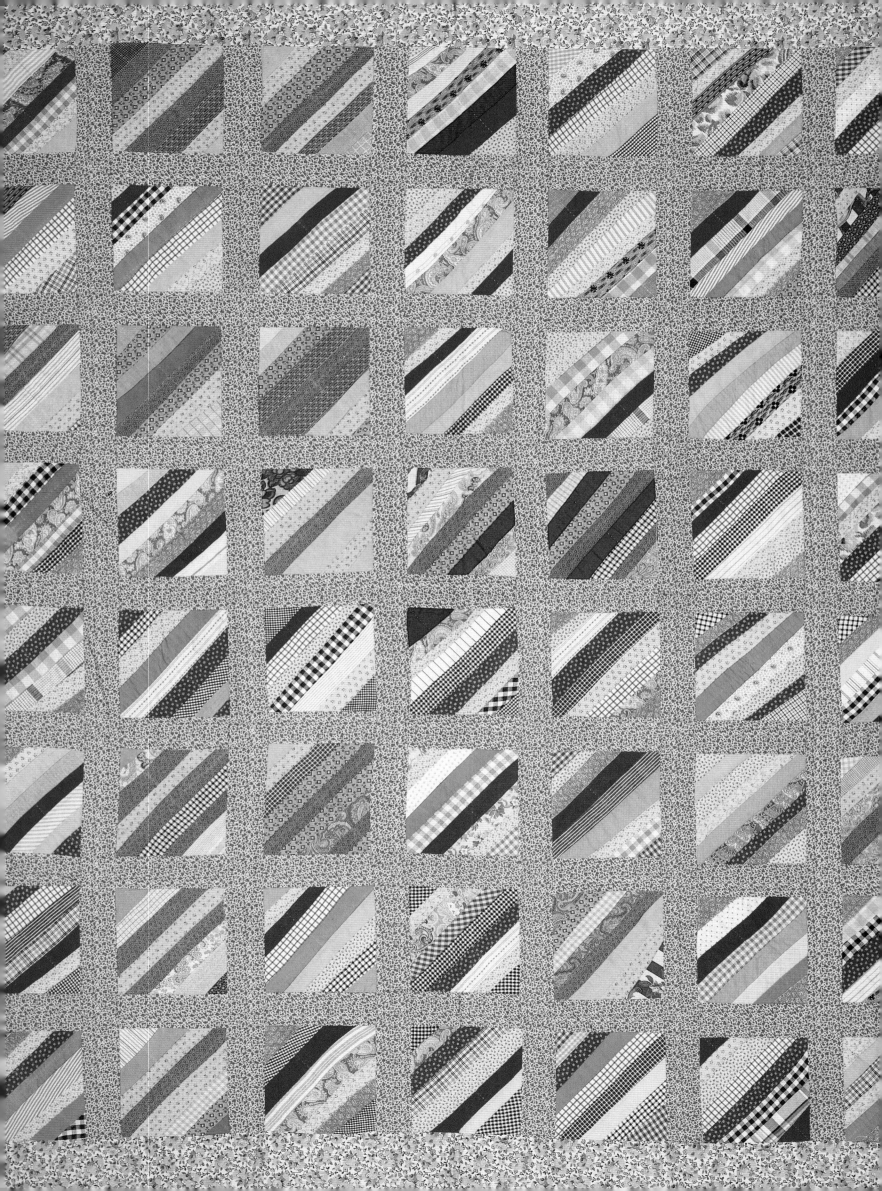

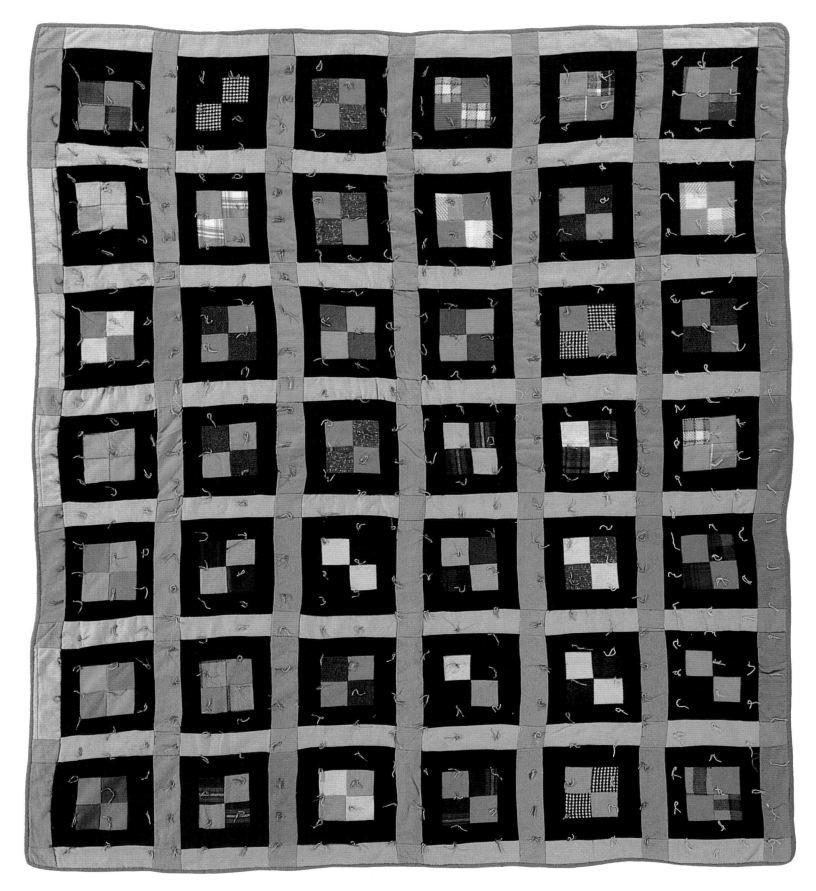

This quilt was made in 1910 in Pennsylvania, pieced together as long "strings" using pattern pieces cut from newsprint.

The greatest number of pieced quilt patterns are variations of Four and Nine Patch designs. The variations of these designs go on endlessly.

The early chintz designs from which the floral appliqués were cut were most likely inspired by the many botanical prints produced in England and Europe. These illustrated the discoveries of the great traveler-naturalists, such as Americans John and William Bartram, who collected plants for English gentleman-gardeners.

their families, including fabric for clothing and home furnishings, while exporting their own goods. Keep in mind that domestic manufacture was not well enough established until the late 1700s to meet demand in quantity, and the cotton gin was not invented until 1793.

The Civil War, which ended in 1865, devastated the South. As Bets Ramsey and Gail Andrews Trechsel recount in *Southern Quilts: A New View*, many areas were heavily looted or completely devastated. Some people could not afford to start over after losing everything they had. Manpower had vanished, families were torn apart, and the economy was nonexistent. It was a bleak time for the region.

During and immediately after the war, fabric was scarce. Quilt makers resorted to using readily available scraps of garments and home-dyed muslin. The habits that they formed during those periods proved long lasting. However, as the South

This combination pieced and appliquéd quilt is almost certainly the original creation of its maker. One would never find this pattern in a book.

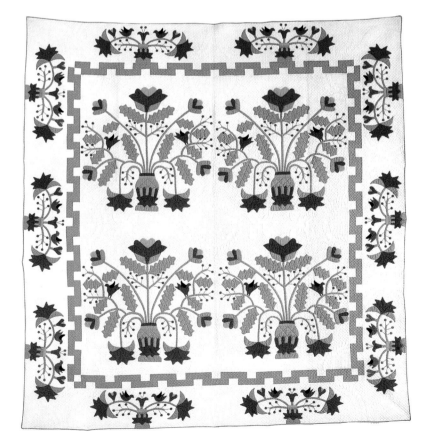

Not all flowers were reproduced from observations of nature. In the latter part of the nineteenth century, commercial patterns became available. Quilters loved to mix different images when creating designs.

Following page: What quilt maker took the time to create this miniature visual wonder? Thousands of tiny squares of fabric from the 1870s were used in the making of this Tumbling Blocks quilt, a true labor of love.

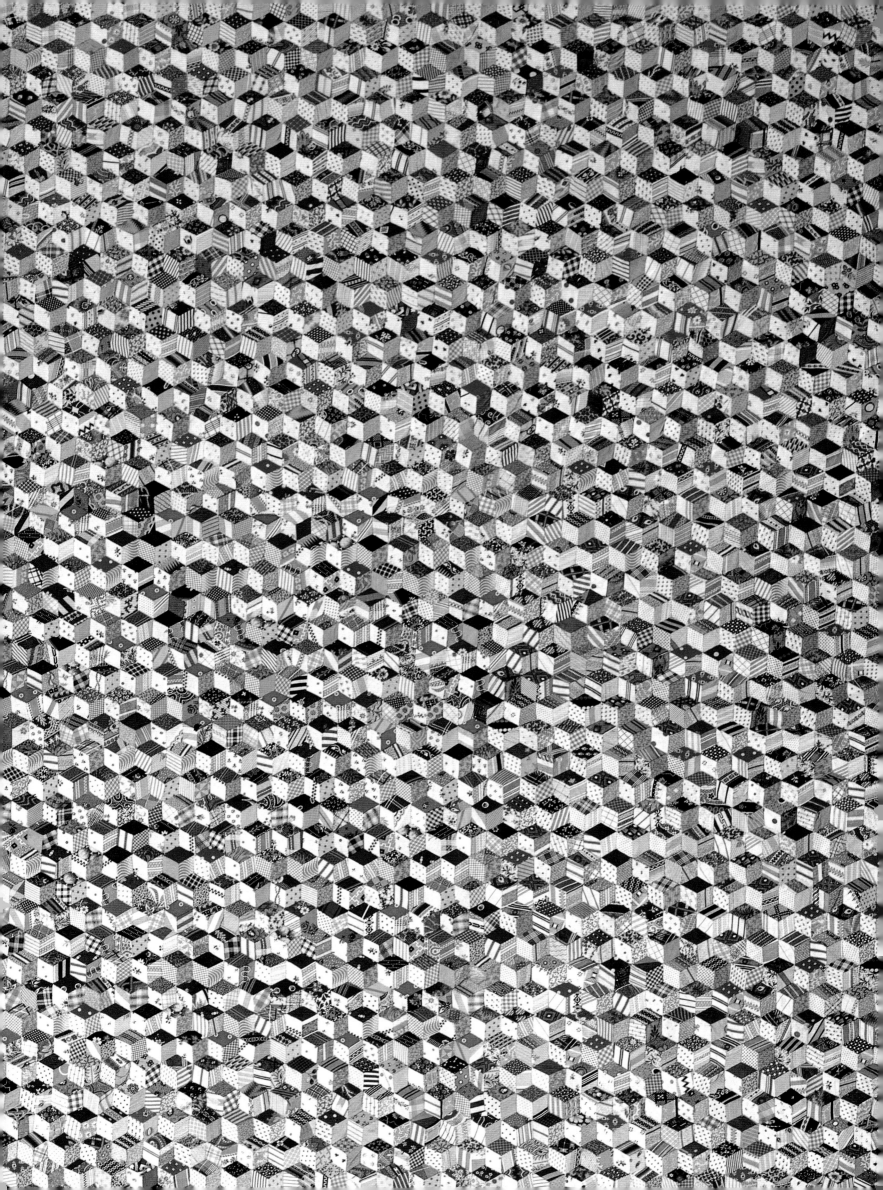

gradually recovered from the war, the agrarian society began to give way to manufacturing and industry, particularly the textile industry, and quilt making flourished, largely because much of the fabric from Southern mills in the late nineteenth century was printed on poor quality cloth and was therefore inexpensive. Virtually all quilters could afford the low retail price. Thus, the backs of Southern quilts were likely to be made of coarse, woven mill cloth or a hand-woven material. The thread used for quilting was usually coarser as well, which resulted in less refined stitching.

During this era, most Southern quilting was done within families. Because of the demands of the rural, agrarian lifestyle and the lengthy travel required between residences in much of the South, day-long quilting bees were rare events.

The popularity of the Crazy quilt swept the South as it did elsewhere in the country. Consisting largely of silks, this type of quilt, was intended as a vehicle to show off the maker's rich collection of textiles and skill as an embroiderer. Silks were more likely found in metropolitan areas while wools were common in more remote places. Perhaps, as Ramsey and Trechsel note, "It cannot be claimed that quilting in the South is distinctly different from that of other places, but certain regional tendencies do seem to exist."[4]

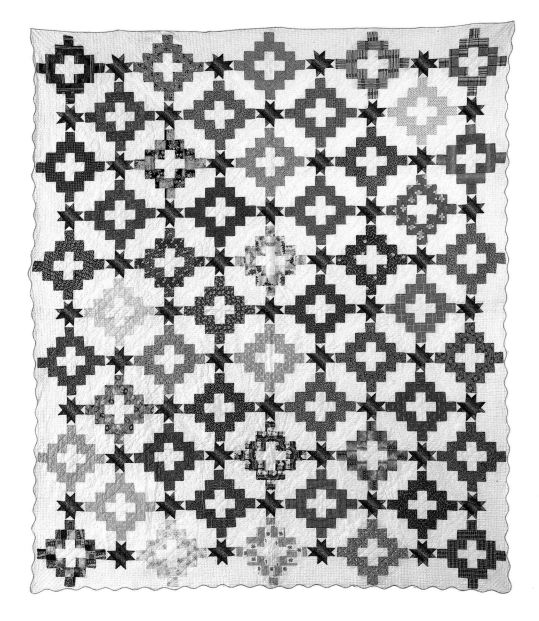

Women often combined patterns in one quilt. This quilt, a combination of Album Patches and pieced Stars, was made in 1870.

VIRGINIA AND THE CAROLINAS

Light colors, especially white, were consistently used in the South because they reflected sunlight (thus reducing heat) and were bright and cheerful. The white whole-cloth quilt without piecing or appliqué was very popular in Virginia and the Carolinas. In fact, white whole-cloth quilts might well have been the favorite form of ornate bed covering prior to the development of the chintz appliqué in the late 1800s, concluded folklorist Laurel Horton.

Chintz appliqué quilts were popular along the Northeast coast and may have inspired some of the beautiful quilts of eastern Tennessee, Kentucky, and North Carolina. Although chintz appliqué quilts were made all over the country, Ramsey and Trechsel feel that "a certain delicacy of line, less vivid color, and regional styles of quilting seem to set some of the southern quilts apart. There are the usual red and green fabrics, but, combined, with pinks and yellows, the impression is less bold than many of the appliqué quilts of the northern states."[5]

In South Carolina, particularly in Charleston, the framed Medallion quilt was quite popular, in large part due to Charleston's status at that time as the largest Southern port. In fact, the "framed center," or Medallion, was the favored pattern of quilters who used chintz fabrics. In areas like Charleston, which had wealthy and style-conscious

*Opposite left:
To create this pattern, the maker often traced the curves with the bottom of a drinking glass.*

*It is not surprising that more than one
hundred known quilt patterns incorporate stars.
The inspiration for them was always present!*

*There are a
variety of bugs
and birds used
in quilt patterns,
both abstract
and realistic.*

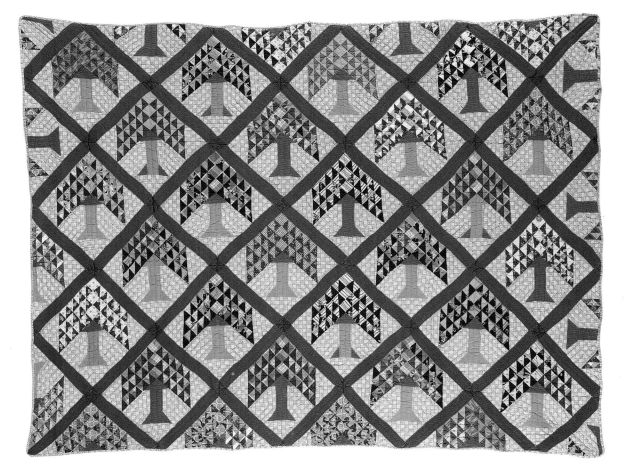

*The pine trees
of New England
inspired this pattern.
The image has a
long history. In 1652
in Massachusetts,
the first coins mint-
ed in the country
had a pine tree
stamped on them.*

residents and easy access to imports, these chintz quilts were very popular. By the second half of the nineteenth century, however, chintz had lost its popularity as the preferred quilt fabric, giving way to solid color and small figured calico fabrics, better suited for creating the intricate geometric patterns that were all the rage. But chintzes continued to be used for borders of quilts in South Carolina and sometimes in quilts made in adjacent areas in North Carolina. The use of chintz in this manner is rarely found in other parts of the country.

Also unique to South Carolina quilt makers was their configuration of a common American pattern called Rocky Mountain Road. In other parts of the country, the pattern was typically set in straight arrangements as well as on the diagonal, but in South Carolina the same pattern was constructed on the vertical-horizontal plane.

The Tree of Life is another distinct pattern that appeared frequently in Virginia and the Carolinas during the Revolutionary period, while the Rose of Sharon pattern was a typical pre-Civil War quilt. The North Carolina documentation project, which began in 1985, repeatedly found "a rosette-like shape appliqued in block design. It seems most likely, because of the prevalence, that the pattern originated there... It was common practice to share patterns with friends afar and seldom did a quilt design remain so isolated as this one had."[6]

This pattern resembles a bear trap. We can only speculate on what inspired the woman who made it.

*Patterns and their names changed as people moved from one part of
the country to another. Designs were frequently re-created from
memory. The earliest patterns certainly belonged to particular localities.*

The center of a quilt did not have to be floral, or pictorial, or even appliquéd. Here, a pieced Star is surrounded by floral broderie perse and has an outer border of chintz carefully chosen to complement the center.

There were never a lot of chintz quilts, mainly because at the height of their popularity, chintz, the key ingredient, was expensive and in short supply. Because chintz quilts were so prized, they were generally saved for "best" and brought out only on special occasions. Since they were so carefully kept, a great many have survived, often in remarkably fine condition.

*Could there be a more charming image of rural life than a pair of doves cooing
on the window sill? Nonetheless, careful choice of fabric transformed this pattern,
embellished with a Nine-Patch Diamond border, into a striking contemporary graphic.*

TENNESSEE AND KENTUCKY

In the late 1760s, a great migration began from Virginia, Maryland, Pennsylvania, and the North in general to the Tennessee wilderness. English, Scotch, Irish, German and, to a lesser extent, African, Dutch, and French immigrants all went to Tennessee looking for land opportunities. These settlers brought with them only their most treasured and important possessions and necessities, along with family traditions and customs. Quilts carried to the settlers' new homes provided a comforting link with family and friends left behind.

Evident from the Tennessee Quilt Project, which began in 1983, was that extraordinary quilts were made in the period immediately preceding the Civil War. Quilt making was viewed as essential preparation for marriage during the antebellum period. The project also examined many quilts made from homegrown materials. These types of materials were used in the nineteenth century as Tennessee was largely an agrarian state that had difficulty in obtaining commercial products. Families had to be virtually self-sufficient. Many households continued to use homemade wool and cotton fabrics even after ready-made batting was widely available.

During the Civil War, Tennessee was a politically divided state (as was Kentucky). It felt the effects of economic depression with the rest of the South. Recovery was prolonged because of scarce resources. Quilts made during this time reflect the impoverished level of Southerners and the sacrifices demanded of them during the postwar period. Many quilts were, out of necessity, made from scrap material.

Household objects were a source of inspiration for quilt patterns and names. This one is called Basket of Scraps.

Even though the patterns of the Tennessee scrap quilts are similar or identical to those made in other states, the difference lies in the fact that elsewhere, cloth was reasonably priced and easily obtained. In contrast, every available household scrap was saved to make Tennessee quilts.

Of the 1,425 quilts documented during the Tennessee Quilt Project, no single type or pattern was found to be unique to Tennessee. Star patterns of every size, shape, and color were the most abundant. One surprising pattern recorded several times during the project, now often associated with Tennessee, was one variously known as Rocky Mountain Road, New York Beauty, Crown of Thorns, Life Everlasting, and Sunset. It is a difficult quilt to make as the cutting must be exact and the piecing accurate.

Other pieced quilt patterns that were found in significant numbers in Tennessee include Snowball, Circles, and various rose patterns, particularly the Rose of Sharon, reflecting the popularity of the Song of Solomon among Victorian young ladies. A further explanation for the abundance of roses in quilts in Tennessee and elsewhere is the significance of the rose as a symbol of simplicity, purity, beauty, love, and bliss.

In their work *The Quilts of Tennessee: Images of Domestic Life Prior to 1930*, Bets Ramsey and Merikay Waldvogel found that Tennessee quilt makers seem to have been inhibited by

The Lady of the Lake pattern is named after Sir Walter
Scott's poem published in 1810. The pattern is found
everywhere in the country and the name has survived.

*A captivating sunburst done in blue,
brown, and gold, this quilt places the viewer
inside the room looking out at the night.*

Thousands of Log Cabin quilts were made in the United States during the 1850s. There were dozens of variations on the pattern. This one is called Streaks of Lightning.

conventionality. Even though nineteenth-century Tennessee quilt makers commonly altered standard patterns to fit their liking, they rarely invented a new one. Another interesting fact that Ramsey and Waldvogel discovered was that the quilts of east Tennessee more resembled the styles of the Carolinas, Virginia, and the North than did those of west and middle Tennessee. However, quilts associated with the older states, such as the Medallion quilts, were scarce in Tennessee. Many east Tennessee quilts can be further identified by their light, clear colors placed on white backgrounds that show a certain elegant flair. West Tennessee quilts, on the other hand, usually consisted of a wider array of solid and printed fabrics and tended to use stronger colors. Even though some of their work was considered crude, many quilters in western Tennessee went to Memphis for choice fabric. Higher quality work and more expensive material was typically found in larger cities.

Much of what can be said about Tennessee holds true of Kentucky. The popularization of the frontier coupled with the scarcity of good land along the seaboard brought many newcomers to both states. The state of Virginia often used frontier lands to pay off Revolutionary soldiers when money was in short supply. Some Tories fled west to escape potential mistreatment and ill feelings in the postwar years. Many settlers from the Middle Atlantic states came

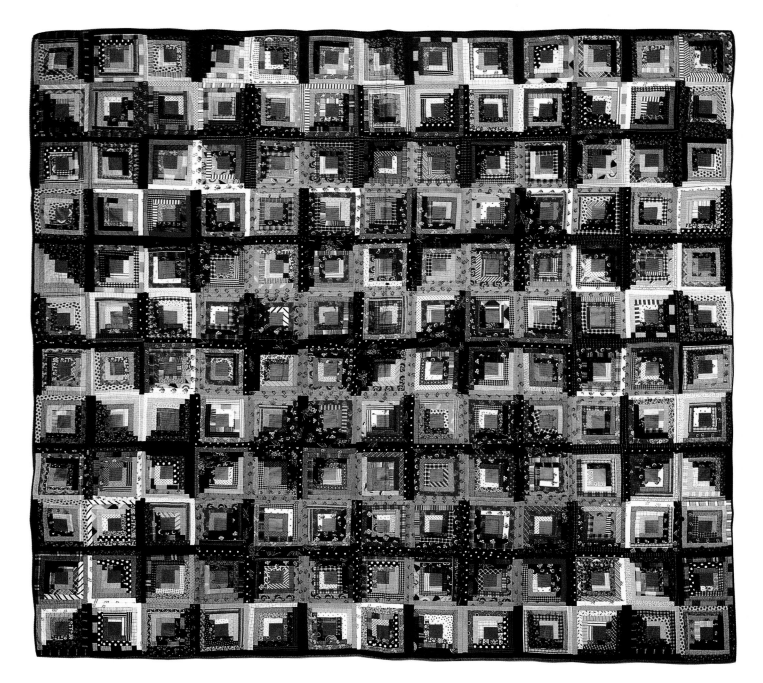

Set on the diagonal, these pieced Carolina Lilies and Suns join forces to create a quilt full of energy.

Made of men's suiting fabrics, this quilt resembles a brick wall. Each block is banded to create the effect of bricks and mortar.

Following page: The Kentucky Sun quilt was the cover quilt for the catalogue Kentucky Quilts 1800-1900, *the first of the state documentation projects, begun in 1981.*

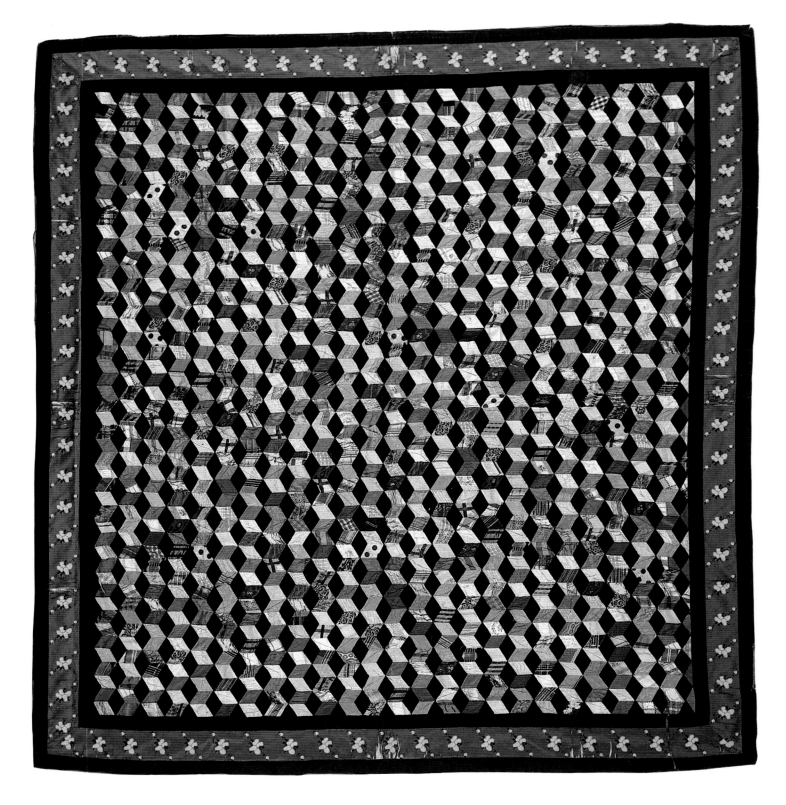

Tumbling Blocks was one of the popular optical designs of the last half of the nineteenth century. This pattern is also known as Baby Blocks. In a quilt of this type, the piecing needs to be exact to produce the desired geometric effect.

to Kentucky by way of the Ohio River, while those migrating from North Carolina and southern Virginia came through the Cumberland Gap. They fanned out across Kentucky and Tennessee over the trails of the Native Americans, which took them into the heart of Kentucky. By the end of the eighteenth century, Kentucky had shed many of the traces of frontier life.

Although it was predominantly an agricultural state, Kentucky had few large plantations. Farmers of fertile bluegrass soil grew wealthy from their crop surpluses, which they shipped to outside markets. Subsistence farmers, on the other

hand, who lived on poorer, more isolated lands, were handicapped by both the lack of easy access to markets and by the varying qualities of soil.

Strategically, Kentucky was in the middle of the Civil War. Tacticians of both South and North knew that Kentucky could affect the outcome of the war. The state, therefore, adopted a neutral position, "Both sides appealed to them, both sides desperately needed them, but Kentuckians, seeking their own way, held back. Lacking the African-American majorities that excited deep racial fears farther south, lacking a militant band of younger slave holders determined on expanding their fortunes, unwilling to abandon

This exquisite quilt, made in Bowling Green, Kentucky, in 1870, could hang in the gallery of the finest art museum.

a tradition of devotion to the Union, realistic about the certainty of armed conflict, Kentucky held back."[7] Both sides ignored Kentucky's neutrality, however, and established bases inside the state. Soldiers on both sides pillaged Kentucky homes. Quilts were prized booty, and women were forced to hide the quilts they had made so painstakingly along with their other valuables.

Among the prized possessions that women might have hidden are the patterns Trip Around the World, Kentucky Rose, and Kentucky Crossroads. Log Cabin quilt designs were favorites with Kentucky quilters. The most popular Log Cabin variations were

Sunshine and Shadows and Barn Raising. The Log Cabin symbolized the spirit of independence and self-reliance. According to Victoria Hoffman, Log Cabin quilts captured the importance of hearth, home, and community. Subtle effects could be achieved through color harmony and by the arrangement of light and dark shades of colors. These manipulations undoubtedly added to the popularity of the pattern, both in Kentucky and elsewhere. Stars, Roses, Lilies, Tulips, and Trees in all variations were also favorite patterns in Kentucky. Kentucky quilters produced few unique masterpieces, but the evidence overwhelmingly suggests that both comfort and beauty were important to the Kentucky quilt maker.

A single pattern was often known by many names. As quilt makers moved West, New York Beauty became Rocky Mountain Road. Crown of Thorns is another name for this pattern, which was popular with quilt makers in Kentucky and Tennessee.

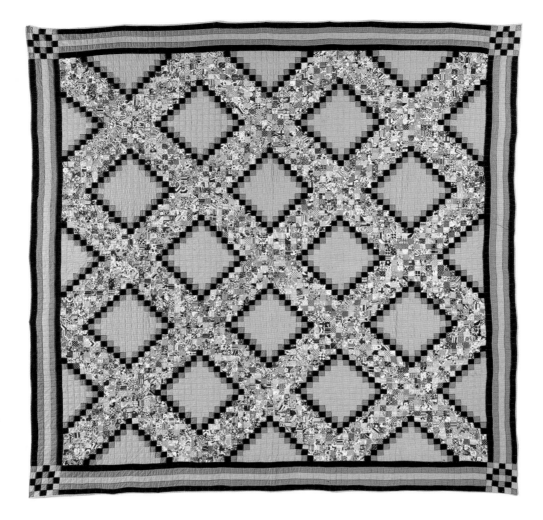

The One Patch was used in many combinations to form multiple types of chains. Postage Stamp chains outlined in black were popular during the 1930s.

TEXAS

Texas was largely settled by Anglo-Americans, primarily from Kentucky and Tennessee. Many of the people who moved to Texas did so because of the Mexican government's offer of low-priced land. As a further enticement, the Mexican government offered free land to men who brought in groups of settlers. In fact, "so enthusiastic were many Kentuckians over Texas that women volunteers were collected and sent to the Southwest to become wives of adventurous single males who had moved there from Kentucky."[8]

Because Texas was basically rural until around the 1930s, as Karoline Patterson Bresenhan and Nancy O'Bryant Puentes note in their book, *Lone Stars: A Legacy of Texas Quilts, 1836-1936*, it was virtually impossible for Texas quilters to purchase manufactured fabrics from any source until the late 1870's. One reason, say Bresenhan and Puentes, was that the homesteads were isolated from each other and often a day's ride from any town or settlement. Also, the fabrics were very expensive. Therefore, Texas women "often resorted to adornment of what they already had on hand. 'Frugality' ruled the life of a Texas quilter [and] challenged her ability to create beauty from leftovers and discards."[9] It is not suprising, therefore, that during the state's quilt project many "instances of hand-woven and home-dyed fabrics [particularly cotton since cotton was the major crop in the state and many quilt makers lived on cotton farms and plantations] used in quilts from 1850 to 1890 were found."[10]

This Star of Chamblie was made from wool suit fabrics at the turn of the century.

Bresenhan and Puentes note that "shades of the sun, the land, the blue of hundreds of miles of open sky, the orange of the Indian paintbrush—these are the colors of the Texas quilter's palette." [11] These were perhaps the most distinguishing aspects of Texas quilts studied in 1983 and 1986 because like those documented in Kentucky and Tennessee, they did not yield stereotypes particular to that state. Certain patterns, however, are commonly associated with Texas, such as the Texas Star, the Texas Rose, the Texas Tulip, and the Texas Yellow Rose.

If you look closely you can see that this is a derivation of a Fan block. Perhaps this unique design was made for Halloween.

*In naming patterns, quilters often made
references to occupations and trades. In this
case a Carpenter's Wheel is suggested.*

*The color range in Ohio Amish
quilts expanded rapidly in
the early twentieth century.*

Appliqué refers to designs cut out and sewn onto a larger piece of fabric. Some of the designs might also have been pieced, as is the case with this quilt.

CHAPTER THREE:

The Midwest

As settlers and immigrants moved west in search of more and better farmland, they took quilts with them both for practical use and as sentimental links to people and places left behind. They served as packing blankets for family treasures, padding for hard wagon seats, and protection from the weather. Because there were not any permanent settlements, new settlers to the Midwest faced many hardships. Self-sufficiency was essential.

As George Knepper notes in *Quilts In Community: Ohio's Traditions*, "Permanent settlement was well underway in the trans-Appalachian West before that part which is now the state of Ohio received its share of the westward migration. ...Years after western Pennsylvania, western Virginia, Kentucky, and Tennessee boasted small wilderness settlements, Ohio remained Indian country." [12]

Though it was a stopover destination for many people migrating west after the War of Independence, a cosmopolitan mixture of people remained in Ohio and settled there. Most of Ohio's population came from New England, the Middle

The Ohio Amish communities were more diverse than those in Lancaster, Pennsylvania. Quilt making reflects the different characteristics of the communities.

Ohio Amish quilt patterns have great variety, complexity, and originality.

Drunkard's Path has been called by many names because there are so many ways to arrange it. It is also known as Old Maid's Puzzle, Love Ring, World Without End, and more. The blocks are a combination of positive and negative space.

Atlantic states, and the upland South. Foreign immigrants who decided to settle in the area brought their own traditions and techniques with them. This added to the richness of life in both Ohio and Indiana. It was during this period that the Amish and Mennonites made their way to Ohio and Indiana, bringing their cultural traditions to the area.

Early settlers in Indiana traveled primarily by the Ohio River and Lake Michigan. In 1811, the United States government started the National Road, a Federal project. It began in Cumberland, Maryland, and extended west. It reached Indiana in the 1830s and became both the primary westward route and an integral part of the local transportation system.

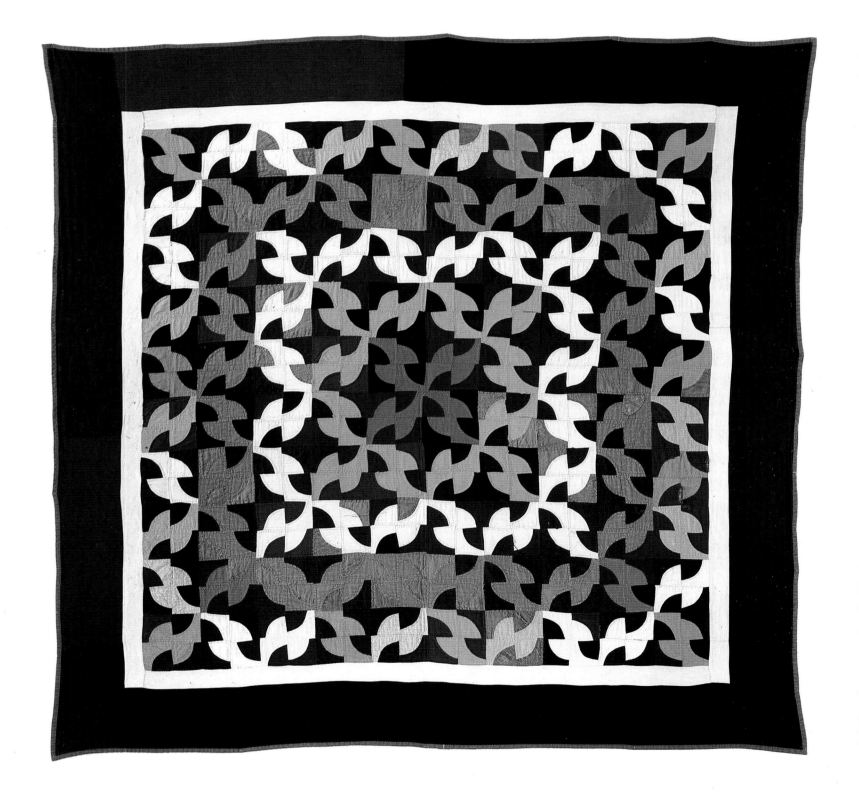

*Broken Dishes uses small triangles, which create a feeling of
movement in the lines of the quilt. Expert piecing and deft handling
of color value and scale are evidence of the quilt's Amish origin.*

Settlement in Kansas occurred much later than in Indiana and Ohio—1854 to be exact, with the frontier period ending in 1880.

This period also marked a significant change in quilt styles, fabric, and quilt pattern dissemination across the country. Synthetic dyes were developed and used to color a growing number of inexpensive cottons. After 1880, mail-order houses sold fabric scraps specifically for quilt making. As a result, similar, if not identical styles proliferated across the country and could be found in households of all economic means.

OHIO

Because textile production increased dramatically in the early nineteenth century, it is not surprising that most of the post-1840 quilts documented by the Ohio Quilt Project, which began in 1984, were made from printed fabrics. Plentiful textiles, better transportation, the availability of the sewing machine, the popularity of certain women's fashions, and the growth of the garment industry all contributed to the increase in quilt making.

In Ohio, quilting styles and patterns spread quickly through quilt-making networks. "The clearest evidence of this was the simultaneous appearance throughout Ohio in the early 1840's of red and green floral appliqué quilts, Ohio's first statewide quilt style. These quilts consisted of a center field of repeated appliquéd blocks, surrounded by a wide border, usually decorated with a vine. Motifs in the blocks were floral; the color scheme was consistently red and green on a white background," often with "details in yellow, orange, or pink, and occasionally, blue." [13] The greatest number of floral appliqués were made between 1840 and 1870. Pieced quilt patterns in nineteenth-century Ohio varied. Two of the most popular were the Ohio Rose and Ohio Star patterns.

The Amish community, which first settled in Ohio in the early nineteenth century, provided another dimension of Ohio quilt making. When the Old Order Amish moved to eastern Ohio, they chose a much more difficult lifestyle than

Appliqué quilt tops are more difficult to make and a majority of quilters consider appliqué quilts to be more beautiful and valuable than pieced ones.

*Sampler quilts show as many patterns as possible. They are sometimes called
Legacy quilts. Sampler quilts were made both by individual quilt makers
and also as a group project in which each person would be assigned a block or
would make one of her own favorite blocks that was then pieced into the whole.*

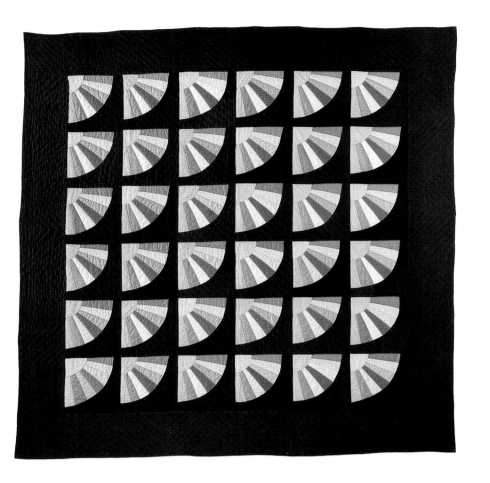

Cotton was the first choice of
fabric for quilt making among
the Ohio Amish. Fan images
are reminiscent of the era when
they were both essential for comfort and significant as ornaments.

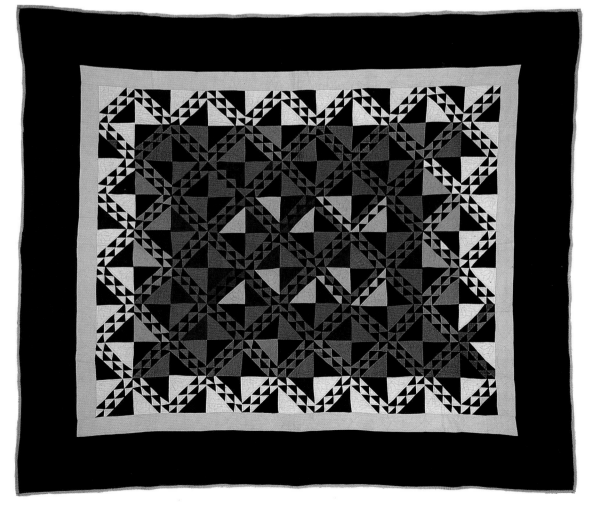

Many Amish quilts
of the Midwest used
saturated color schemes.
Black backgrounds
were popular between
the 1920s and 1940s.

that which they had left behind in Pennsylvania. Yet this did not stop the flow of Amish families to Ohio from Pennsylvania. Many European Amish and Mennonites also moved to Ohio, adding to both numbers and diversity.

According to Eve Wheatcroft Granick, the originality and complexity of the Ohio Amish quilts are striking. The Ohio Amish developed a large body of designs, from the simplest to the most intricate. Moreover, as she notes in *The Amish Quilt*, "patterns were not limited to a central, single, or even traditional design. ...Inside and outside borders were sometimes enhanced by diamonds, sawtooths, zigzags, and keyboard piecework. Sawtooth bindings and bindings pieced out of several different colors also appear." [14] In addition, they designed both the fronts and backs of their quilts. Many quilts had a pieced design on one side and a plain border design on the other.

Unlike their Pennsylvania cousins, says Granick, Ohio Amish quilts display a variety of standard piecework patterns, and even a few rare examples of appliqué designs. Some were popular only at certain times or within particular areas. Generally speaking, the following patterns enjoyed lasting popularity: Baskets, Sunshine and Shadow, Log Cabin, Nine Patch, Railroad Crossing, Bars, and Ocean Waves. In contrast to the subdued palette of Lancaster County, Pennsylvania, Ohio Amish used almost every conceivable color in their quilts. Granick further notes that some quilts are quite plain and simple, with one color for the background and one or two contrasting colors for the inside borders and binding. Block quilts of two colors were another popular form. Typical colors of the backgrounds of Ohio Amish quilts in the nineteenth century and early twentieth century were blue, brown, or red. Black backgrounds, although characteristic of Ohio Amish quilts, are not found until the 1920s and 1940s.

Not all quilts express frugality, but every quilt reflects self-sufficiency. The quilter, whatever her station or design, combines her materials, skills, and imagination to create a useful object out of disparate fragments.

Granick believes that "quilts made in the Ohio Amish districts reflect a distinctly different type of community from those in Lancaster or the smaller eighteenth- and nineteenth-century Pennsylvania settlements. In Ohio the Amish found enough land and a particular type of geography to permit various church districts and factions to develop their own way of life without the stress of enforced geographic proximity." [15] Amish life was much more liberal in many Ohio communities than in Pennsylvania.

*In this original version of the Hexagon, the applied border
keeps the blocks from appearing to leap off the quilt.*

*The Irish Chain is one of the oldest block patterns. It evolved from one basic shape,
the square, used for both pieces and blocks. It can be arranged in many variations.*

*In the quilts of any period, you will see
extremes of frugality and extravagance.*

*The subtle effects achieved by color harmony and the
contrast of light and dark shades effectively have undoubtedly
contributed to the popularity of Log Cabin quilts.*

INDIANA

Early Indiana quilts were much like their Ohio neighbors. Green and red appliqué quilts with white background predominated and often had touches of orange, pink, or chrome yellow. Appliquéd quilts frequently featured flowers, particularly the rose, which appeared in various forms, including the Rose of Sharon, Ohio Rose, and Indiana Rose. The Indiana Quilt Project, which began in 1986, concluded that Star patterns of all sizes and shapes were also popular.

By the mid-nineteenth century, pieced quilts had become more numerous, and scrap quilts were coming of age. Popular patterns included the Indiana Wreath, Indiana Puzzle, and Indiana Farmer.

In the 1840s many Old Order Amish families moved to Indiana from Pennsylvania and Ohio. Additionally, immigrants from European Amish and Mennonite communities in Switzerland, Alsace, and southern Germany also came to Indiana. There were many pressures and conflicts during these years because of the impending schism between the Old Order Amish and the Mennonites. Therefore, the Amish communities in Indiana were even more diverse than those in Ohio. Indiana still has the third largest community of Old Order Amish in the United States.

The Drunkard's Path, a pattern that swerves and meanders across the quilt, was intended to teach moral lessons. It is also called Pumpkin Vine.

Some Amish families, like other Americans, took part in the migration westward to farmlands that had opened for settlement in the eighteenth and early nineteenth centuries. Life was more difficult in the Midwest than it had been in the more established Lancaster County, Pennsylvania, area.

The String quilt was a popular design for using up extra scraps of cloth. No quilter considers a String quilt a showpiece, yet some, like this one, are quite beautiful.

Like the Ohio neighbors, Amish settlers in Indiana were faced with the task of building their community from the ground up. There were few differences between Indiana and Ohio Amish quilts during the late nineteenth and early twentieth centuries. Granick found some unique Indiana Amish quilt patterns did appear. The Fan design was one of those patterns, particularly popular in Indiana during the first thirty years of the twentieth century. The Fan quilt was rarely found in Pennsylvania or Ohio. Other popular Indiana Amish quilt patterns were Shoo-fly, Log Cabin, Baskets, Bow Ties, and Nine Patch variations.

The popular colors used in early Indiana Amish quilts included rich burgundy, deep golden yellow, orange, and indigo blue. These were not as popular in Ohio quilts. Colors

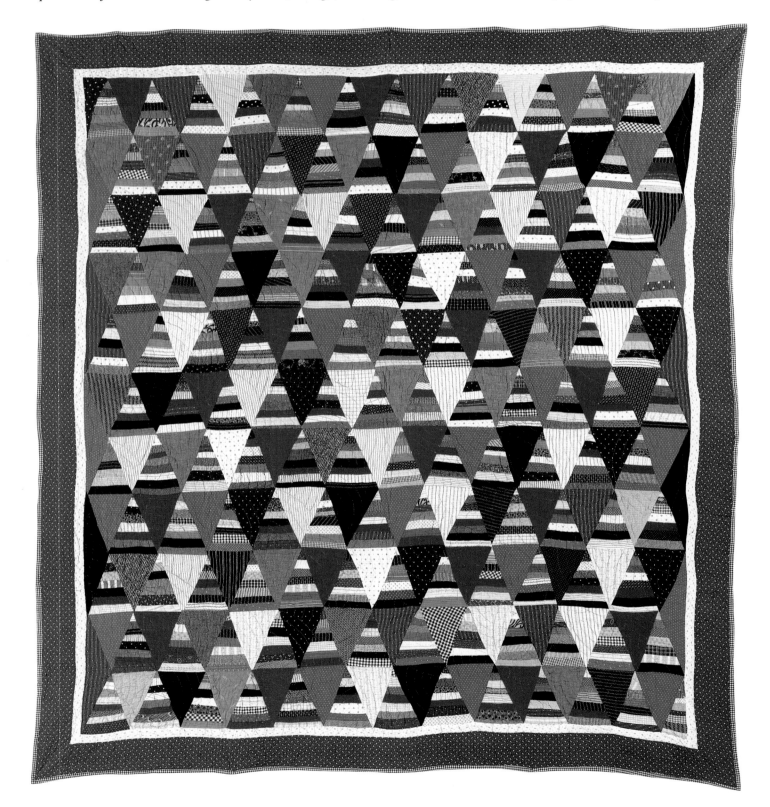

used by both communities in both states included blues, browns, tans, and greens. Throughout the Amish communities of Pennsylvania, Ohio, and Indiana, color was distinctive. Granick says that the Indiana Amish used strong red in their quilts and occasionally some printed fabrics, unlike their Ohio neighbors who overwhelmingly used solid colors. Indiana Amish also made blue and white quilts between 1920 and 1940, but these were not very popular. For the most part the traditions of both the Ohio and Indiana Amish were similar, each affected by the prosperity and stability of their communities and their migration patterns. Because the Amish Midwest communities tended to be more liberal, they were more susceptible to English and Mennonite influences than they would have been had they remained in more conservative Pennsylvania Amish Communities.

This Nine Patch Bow Tie is a delightful pattern. The bow ties seem to be dancing across the surface of the quilt.

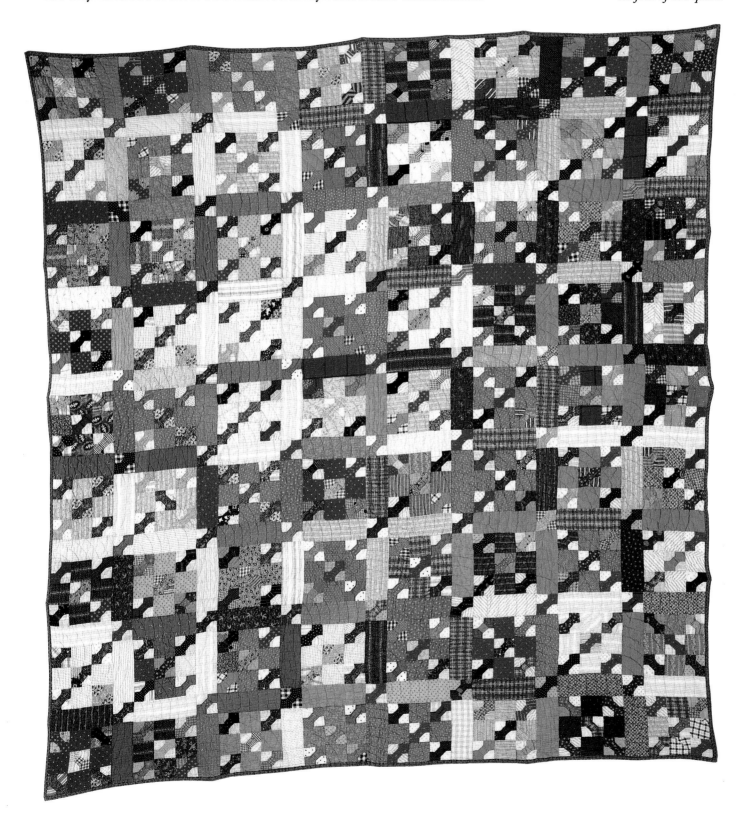

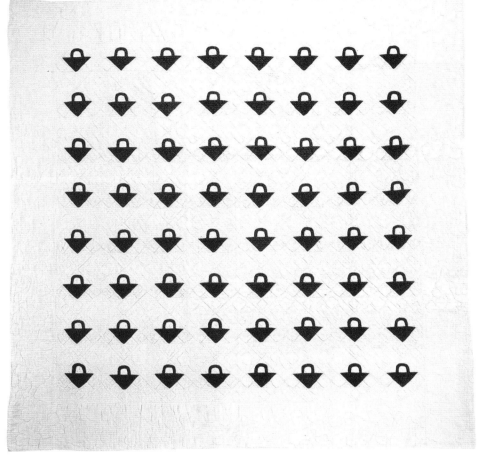

This primitive Baskets quilt is an interesting contrast to other, more complex designs of this type. This one is like a delicate pencil sketch.

This quilt is an encyclopedia of fabrics of the 1870s. The maker, as often is the case, is unknown, but the technique and color sense are extraordinary.

KANSAS

Most Kansas settlers were young families looking for a new life after the Civil War. They were drawn to Kansas by the availability of free land. Few women lived in Kansas during the early years of settlement. These were decades when quilt making was popular in America both out of necessity and for reasons of socialization. In fact, Virginia, New York, and Ohio, the three most populous states in 1860, had twenty times more women than Kansas.

Kansas became known for its "sod houses." Settlers never intended, when they left the civilized East, to live their lives in a hole in the ground in order to survive drought, grasshopper plagues, and blizzards. But there were no forests on the Plains, and thus, no timber with which to build shelters.

Kansas had virtually no textile manufacturing capabilities or operations. Quilt fabrics were either imported from the East or Europe. Pioneer women might have produced their own fabrics, but the Kansas Quilt Project found no evidence of this, probably because by the time Kansas was open to settlement, homespun fabric was rapidly being supplanted by cheap cottons manufactured in New England's thriving textile industry.

The settlement of Kansas parallels the development of popular quilt making in the United States, but few of the more than thirteen thousand quilts documented by the Kansas Quilt Project were found to be true Kansas quilts. Most were transplants. There were few, if any, significant differences between the quilts of Kansas and those of the eastern United States up until 1880.

Ironically, it seems, Kansas influenced the names of quilt patterns more than any other state. Before commercial pattern companies and newspaper columns began renaming traditional patterns, there were a few nineteenth-century patterns named for Kansas. For example, Rocky Road to Kansas may have been named by immigrants who traveled along the Oregon and Santa Fe Trails, which brought settlers to the state after 1854. Kansas Troubles reflects the hardships that the settlers encountered upon arrival, and Kansas Dugout refers to settlers who started their lives in Kansas literally living in a hole in the ground. Kansas Beauty reflects the settlers' growing love for the beauty of their state as plantings and farms prospered.

There are many speculations as to why there are not more Kansas-made quilts. Barbara Brackman has postulated that there may have been little need to make quilts in the early years of settlement because people brought with them an ample supply of quilts and bedding, thus women were freed up to produce other needed items. Another theory is that the quilts simply may have been used up, worn out, and discarded. Until the coming of the railroad, fabric was scarce in Kansas. Cotton was grown only in a few counties in

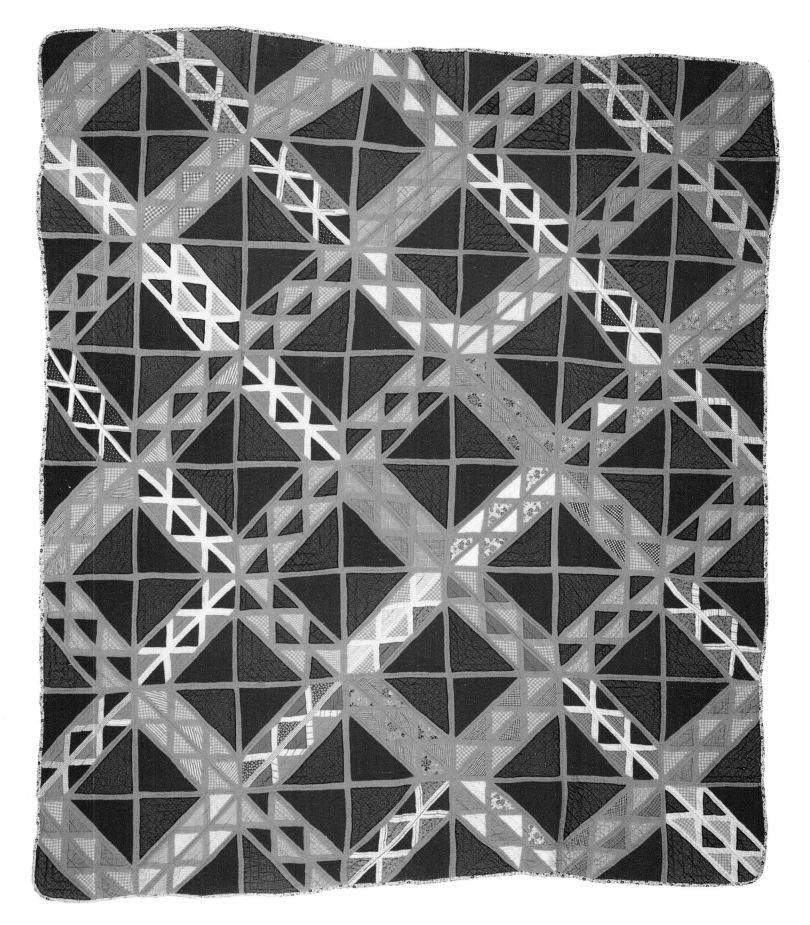

The family's store of corn and beans saw them and their livestock through a hard winter. Barrels of colorful dried grains and legumes provided the inspiration for this quilt.

the southern section of the state and textile manufacturing never really established itself. In addition, it must be considered that quilts documented by the Kansas Quilt Project were predominantly the types meant to be saved and not actual Kansas-made quilts, which for the most part were cruder and more utilitarian. Because Kansas-made quilts were frontier quilts, they were probably thicker, coarser, warmer, and quickly put together because of time and material limitations. They may have been made to be used and thrown out. Only further research can unveil the enigma of Kansas-made quilts.

Following page: There are many Star quilt patterns. Perhaps this fascination with the sky comes from the fact that much of rural life is ruled by the sun and heavens.

The unlikely color combinations of this quilt were used successfully by its Pennsylvania maker. The Pennsylvania Germans loved strong color.

*Pine Tree, or Tree of Paradise, was one of
the earliest American quilt patterns to reflect the
importance of trees in the development of this land.*

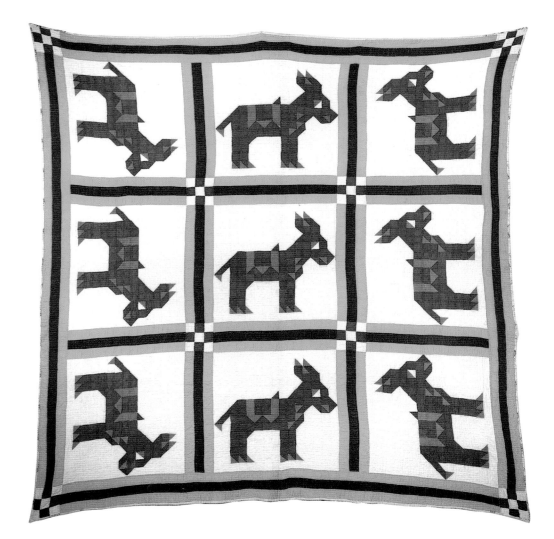

Many quilts were made to express political beliefs. Certainly a good Democrat made this one.

CHAPTER FOUR:

The Far West

Between 1841 and 1866, over 350,000 people, including thousands of families, migrated westward toward the Pacific seeking land and fortunes in gold. The eastern section of the United States was experiencing economic recession as well as population expansion.

Quilts, like the settlers themselves, were exposed to weather conditions, attack, injury, and illness. All facets of wagon-train life—births, illnesses, injuries and deaths—involved the use of quilts. The weather conditions and rocky, wet terrain posed a threat to fabrics as well as to people. Many families slept in the open on bedding under or near their wagon trains for shelter. It is difficult to believe that so many quilts survived the rugged, hazardous trip west. It shows the loving care the quilts received, as well as their durability.

Pioneers heading west had a sense of adventure and enthusiasm. Some left behind families and set out on their own. Women, especially those who lost their husbands during the hazardous trip west, became stronger and self-reliant. They broke the ties to the East, whether joyfully or with regret, leaving behind their

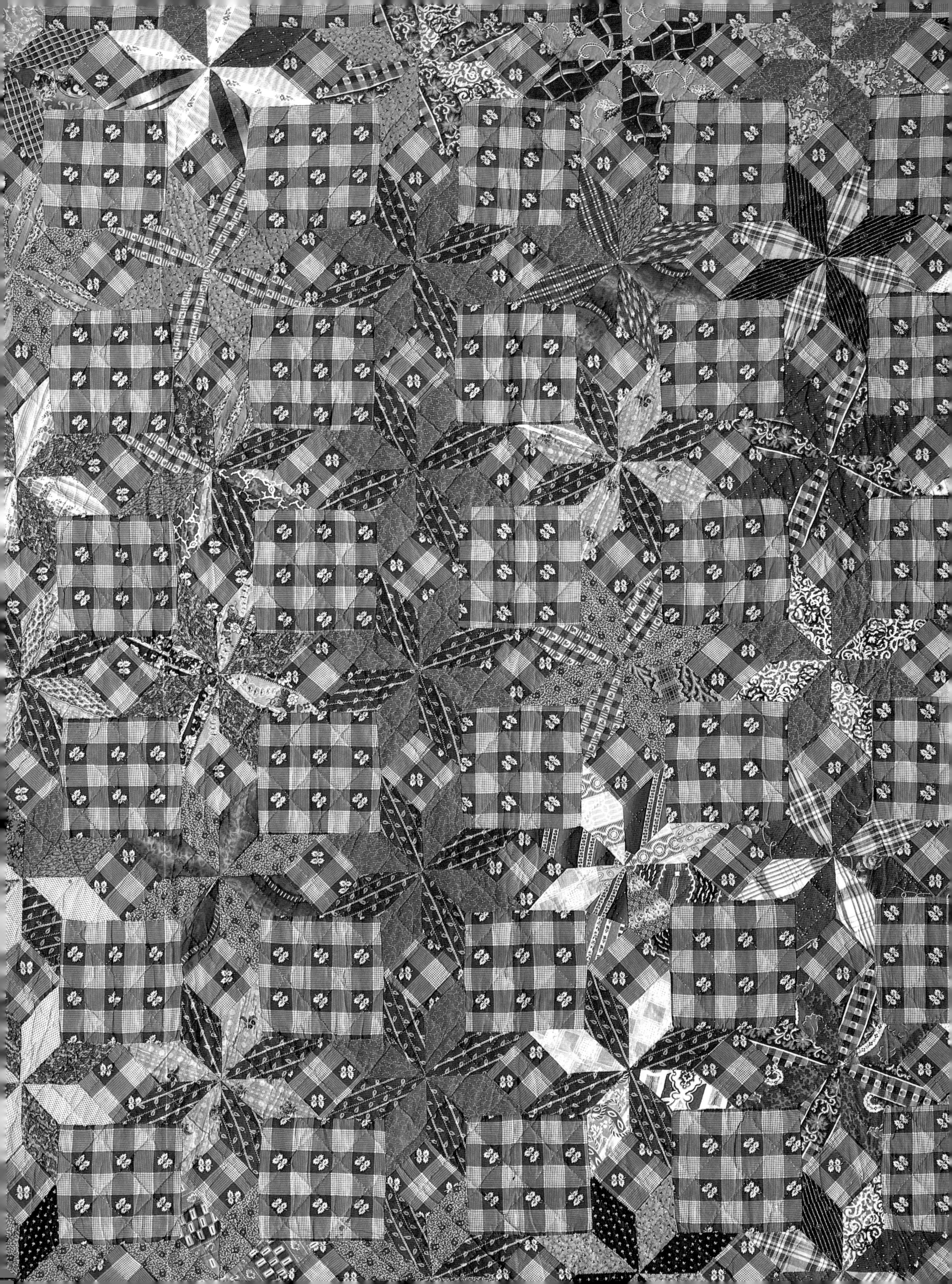

communities and support networks of family and friends. They soon experienced the freedom that came with greater responsibility. The forging of new viewpoints, new lifestyles, and new human connections no doubt affected their quilt designs.

Women moving to the West often felt disconnected from familiar people and environments. Typically, they moved from the East Coast to the Mississippi Valley, then continued the journey westward. Treasured friendships were sacrificed with each move, and were often captured in many of the friendship quilts taken west. Women, whether Asian, European, Hispanic, or American, quickly took on more active roles in their new, prospering communities. These roles were not only needed, but welcomed. The women were depended upon to maintain continuity with the life they had left behind and the new lives they had just begun. Their quilts often reflected the new lives of these transplanted women.

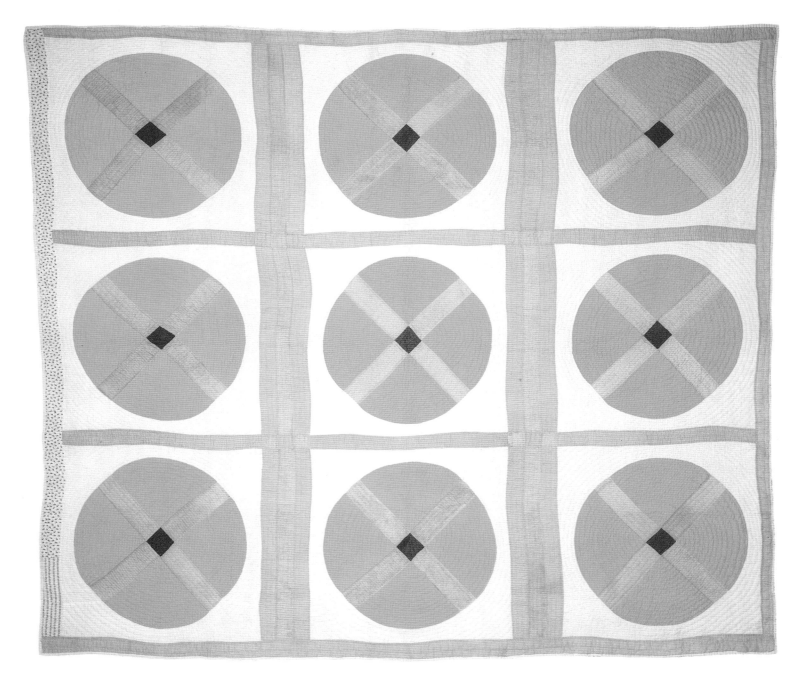

Stars are the favorite pattern of many quilt makers. Pattern names proliferate and overlap, reemerging as they show minor variations under new and old names.

This quilt hung in the lobby of the Whitney Museum of American Art in New York in 1971. It was the banner quilt for the exhibition "Abstract Design in American Quilts."

Crazy quilts became popular in the Victorian era when fashion tended toward excess. A Crazy quilt is constructed by overlapping irregularly shaped pieces of cloth and then embellishing every seam with elaborate embroidered stitches. The individual pieces were often also stitched or painted with names, initials, dates, flowers, and other images.

CALIFORNIA

Once California was admitted to statehood in 1850, the cities of Sacramento and San Francisco quickly took on the characteristics of many of the cosmopolitan cities of the East. Rural areas enjoyed prosperity because of the cultivation of wheat, hay, fruit, and rice. The railroad's arrival enhanced both the rural and urban economies. In 1869, the completion of the transcontinental railroad and the Suez Canal that same year would only enhance the future prosperity of California.

According to Jean Ray Laury in *Ho for California! Pioneer Women and Their Quilts*, "no indigenous style typifies early California quilts. The diverse approaches and styles brought West were tumbled together in new communities. Diversity itself became a trait. Quilts were often pieced in order to maintain traditions and reestablish the values of a home life left behind. The quilting activity itself offered continuity, but the California move interrupted local influences on quilters' traditional work."[16] Thus we find such patterns as California Rose, California Star, California Oak Leaf, California Bungalow, California Plume, and Rocky Road to California.

The Princess Feather design was adapted from the Prince of Wales' plumes and was a popular mid-nineteenth century pattern.

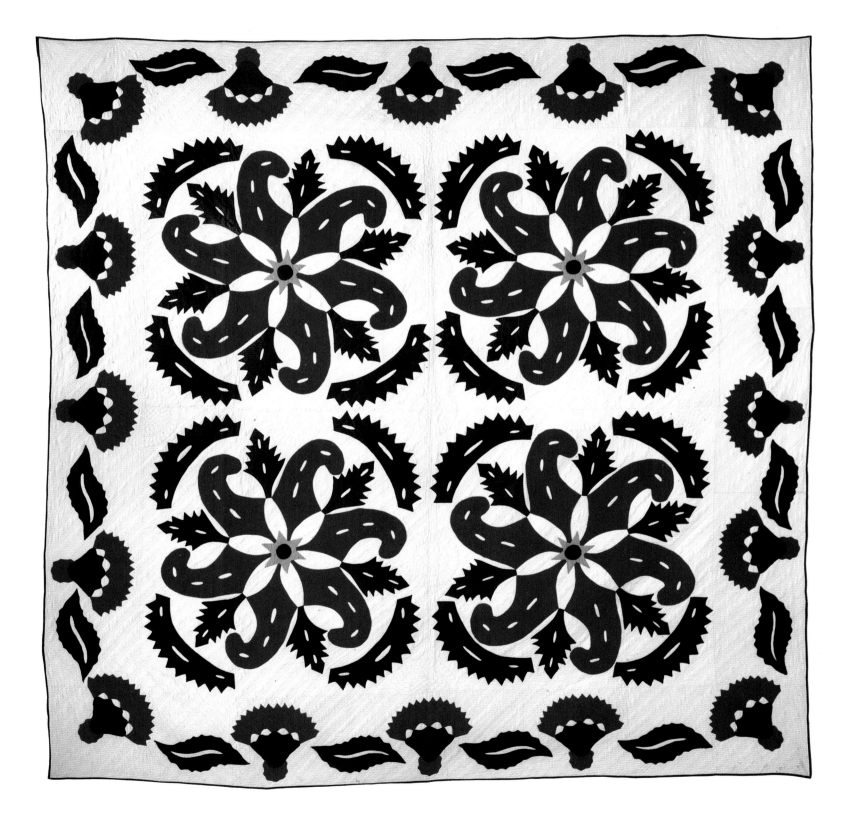

Different ways of constructing the Log Cabin blocks and varied techniques for setting them together allowed the quilter a lot of room for creativity. As utility quilts in wools and cottons, as scrap quilts mixing fabrics, or as silk and velvet quilts for parlor throws and keepsakes, Log Cabins were among the most colorful and interesting patterns.

OREGON

Oregon became a state in 1859, fifteen years after the first settlers arrived there. Crossing overland on the Oregon Trail, immigrants went in search of land and gold, and on their last few days of the journey they would have been awestruck by Mount Hood, the highest point in the Cascade Mountain Range. They would have also felt relief when they saw Oregon's forests after days of crossing the western deserts.

Several Oregon patterns, such as Oregon Trail, derived their names from the settlers' experiences. It is not clear, however, how long this design has been called Oregon Trail by quilt makers. The makers of these quilts were probably not the same women who rode in wagons and walked the trail, since most were made after 1880, when railroads were the primary source of westward travel. Women probably made few quilts while on the trail, due to the rigors of the trip. Related patterns telling of the experience include Wagon Tracks and Lewis and Clark.

The technique and pattern of this quilt demonstrate ingenious adaptations rather than unique conceptions. Most experienced quilters have tried at least one novelty quilt and each has preferences in materials and patterns.

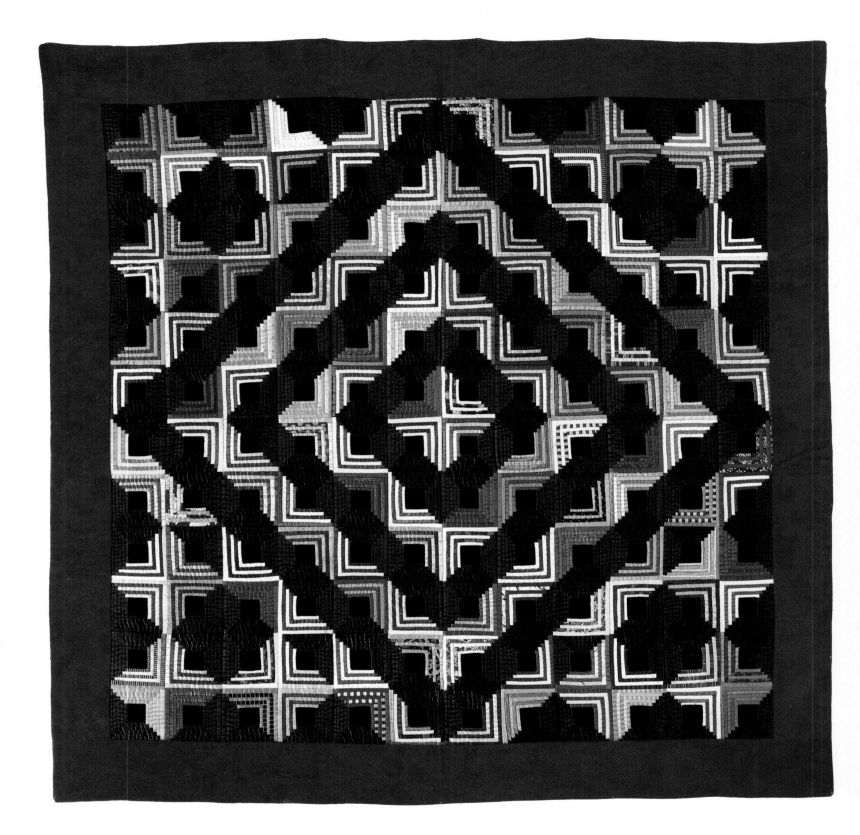

*The Log Cabin pattern first became popular
in the 1850s and its popularity continues today.
It was identified with rugged pioneer ideals.*

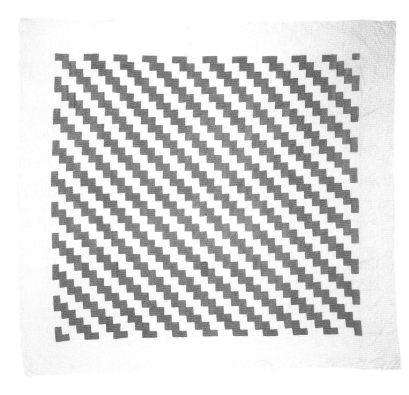

This Streak of Lightning quilt represents what a quilt maker might have seen in the sky during a storm.

Made from a Fan block, this quilt, because of its form and coloration, looks like it was made in the West.

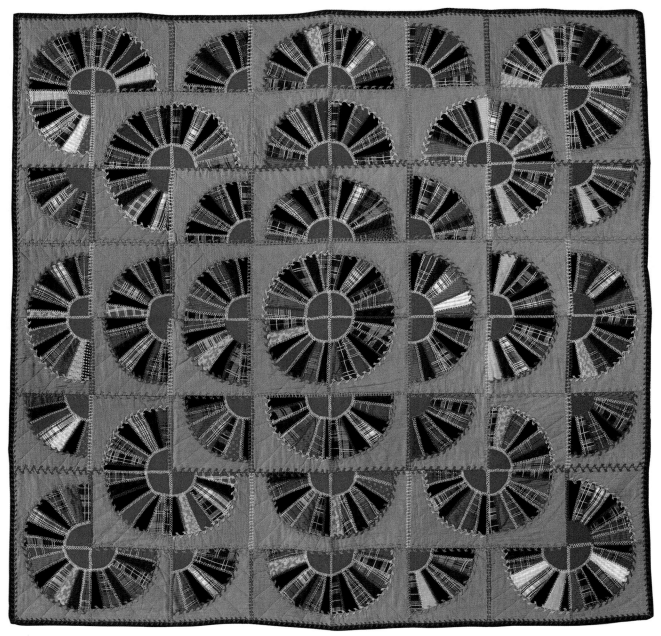

HAWAII

Hawaii's story is different from any other state in America. It became the fiftieth state, but not until 1959, and it was settled first not by New Englanders or European or Mexican immigrants, but by Polynesians who arrived from elsewhere in the Pacific. European colonists did not arrive until late in the 1770s.

Hawaiian quilts are distinctive both in patterns and names. According to Patsy and Myron Orlofsky, authors of *Quilts in America*, the "technique of patchwork was introduced to the islands during the first quarter of the nineteenth century by the wives of missionaries. The use of needle and thread was new to the women of Hawaii and instruction in sewing became part of the curriculum in missionary schools." [17] In their evolution, Hawaiian quilts bore no resemblance in design to the mainland pieced quilts, though there is a relationship to appliqué styles. Hawaiian homes had no scrap bags for materials, and full widths of cloth were used to cut clothing, leaving no wasted material. Hawaii's isolation from the mainland, combined with its residents' strong native

tradition, created a distinctive style of quilting that still survives.

Early Hawaiian quilt patterns typically consisted of a central turkey-red pattern on a white background, with the motif repeated over the top. Other colors were eventually used along with turkey red, but quilters continued to prefer a single color on a white background. Hawaiian quilting generally follows the outlines of the pattern.

Hawaiian quilters were very interested in quilt patterns, and the creator of a design was given the honor of naming it. Hawaiian women drew upon the natural beauty of the islands for their designs, resulting in pattern names such as Breadfruit, Rose Wreath, and Lei Mamo.

Hawaii is also known for its red, white, and blue Royal Hawaiian Flag Quilts. These stunning, rare quilts date from approximately 1845. Each stripe represents a major island. Today, owners of Hawaiian quilts are reluctant to publicize these mysterious symbols of a lost kingdom, explaining why so few Royal Hawaiian Flag quilts have made their way to the mainland.

Stella Jones, a pioneer in the study of Hawaiian quilts, refers to Ku'u Hai Aloha (My Beloved Flag) as the most beloved Hawaiian quilt design. "Upon abdication of the queen and the consequent lowering of their flag, many of the Hawaiian people feared they would not again be permitted to fly the emblem of their kingdom. They turned to the quilt as a means of perpetuating the flag and coat of arms, and the result was My Beloved Flag, a design held so sacred as never to be put to common use."

Hawaiian legend tells us that picking a Lehua blossom will bring the rain. Many of the quilts made with this design have come to us from the "big island" of Hawaii.

Though quilters sometimes share or copy designs, they usually create new names for each of their quilts. Hawaiian quilts are usually named for the spirit of its design.

This quilt was made for Queen Liliuokalani, the last monarch of Hawaii. The quilt is most unusual in that center and border designs are connected and the white fabric is used as the appliqué. It is believed that the quilt was made on the "big island" of Hawaii.

This quilt was made by Mary Kaulahao and was originally inspired by the etched glass doors of the Iolani Palace. Perhaps this design represented a way for a quilter to capture a precious moment in her life.

*Following page:
Tumbling Blocks are not identified with any specific area of the country. Patterns were taken by settlers moving from the east to their new homes in the West.*

*It was once believed that if a single girl made a Lone Star
quilt she would become an old maid. Despite this superstition,
Lone Stars were one of the most popular quilt patterns.
The design uses straight-sided geometric pieces to form blocks.
It is also known as Star of Bethlehem and Star of the East.*

The symbol of the order of the Eastern Star,
one of the many secular societies popular
in this country, is the theme of this quilt.

Afterword

The word "quilt" conjures up many images in people's minds, including warmth, security, comfort, and home. But since 1971—the beginning of the most recent quilt revival—quilts have come to mean much more. They are appreciated for their artistic and creative beauty, much as paintings are appreciated, and have moved from the bed to the wall, often replacing paintings as the preferred artwork for many individuals, corporations, and public institutions. Quilts are now recognized and studied as historical, social, and cultural records of the people who settled this nation. Increasingly quilt history serves to enhance understanding and study of American life.

Great American art quilts have been made in the past, some clearly meant never to be used as bed covers. But only in the recent decades have a group of men and women thought of themselves as artists first and artisans second. Shown here is From the Nine Patch to the Future by Marla M. Hattabaugh, dating from 1985-6.

The inspiration for this quilt, made by quilt artist
Tom Cuff in 1990, was the traditional pattern Robbing Peter
to Pay Paul. This is one of the ways in which contemporary
quilt artists pay homage to earlier quilt-making traditions.

In the 1970s, quilts began to be studied and exhibited as a design phenomenon. Many ensuing exhibitions, with their accompanying publicity, revived a general interest in quilts. Since then there has been a phenomenal interest in quilts worldwide. A body of highly accomplished contemporary artists has chosen quilt making as its medium. Art galleries here and abroad show their work alongside that of painters and sculptors. American Bison Spirit Heritage Quilt (1985), depicted here, was created by Hilary Ervin of Waterville, Maine.

Appendix

STATE PATTERN NAMES

The following is a list of representative pattern names from various states:

Alabama	Alabama Beauty
Alaska	Alaska Chinook, Alaska Homestead
Arizona	Arizona's Cactus Flower
Arkansas	Arkansas Star, Arkansas Traveler, Arkansas Centennial, Arkansas Crossroads, Arkansas Diamond, Arkansas Meadow Rose, Arkansas Troubles
California	California Oak Leaf, California Rose, California Snowflake, California Star, California Poppy, California Sunflower, California Bungalow, Rocky Road to California, California Plume
Colorado	Colorado Columbine, Colorado Beauty, Colorado Star, Colorado's Arrowhead, Pikes Peak, Rocky Mountain
Connecticut	Connecticut, Connecticut Star, Tobacco Leaf
Delaware	Delaware Crosspatch, Delaware's Flagstones, Hens and Chicks
Florida	Florida Forest, Florida Star, Key West Beauty, Key West Star
Georgia	Savannah Beautiful Star, Cherokee Rose, Cotton Blossom, Confederate Rose, Sherman's March, Marietta Blockhouse, Peach Blow, Cracker, Live Oak Tree
Hawaii	Breadfruit, Rose Wreath, Lei Mamo
Idaho	Idaho Star, Idaho Beauty
Illinois	Illinois Star, Illinois Road, Illinois Turkey Track, Chicago Star
Indiana	Indiana Farmer, Indiana Puzzle, Indiana Rose

Iowa	Iowa Rose, Iowa Wreath, Iowa Star	North Dakota	North Dakota
Kansas	Kansas Troubles, Rocky Road to Kansas, Kansas Beauty, Kansas Dugout, Kansas Dust Storm, Kansas Star, Kansas Sunflower	Ohio	Ohio Star, Ohio Rose, Cleveland Lilies, Cleveland Tulip, Cincinnati Dog Wheel, Pride of Ohio
Kentucky	Kentucky Beauty, Kentucky Crossroads, Kentucky Rose, Kentucky Chain, Trip Around the World, Log Cabin	Oklahoma	Oklahoma Star, Oklahoma Sunburst, Oklahoma Twister, Oklahoma Square Dance, Oklahoma Dogwood, Oklahoma Trails and Fields
Louisiana	Louisiana Star	Oregon	Oregon Trail, Wagon Tracks, Lewis and Clark
Maine	Maine		
Maryland	Maryland Beauty, Annapolis Star, Baltimore Belle	Pennsylvania	Pennsylvania Rose, Star of Bethlehem, Philadelphia Beauty, Philadelphia Pavement
Massachusetts	Boston Commons, Boston Corners, Boston Pavement, Boston Puzzle	Rhode Island	Rhode Island Maple Leaf Star
Michigan	Michigan Beauty, Michigan Star, Lansing, Cherry Wreath, Pine Tree	South Carolina	Rocky Mountain Road, South Carolina
Minnesota	Minnesota	South Dakota	South Dakota
Mississippi	Mississippi Daisy, Mississippi Oak Leaf, Mississippi Star	Tennessee	Tennessee Circle, Tennessee Star, Tennessee Tulip, Tennessee Snowball, Rocky Mountain Road, Rose of Sharon
Missouri	Missouri Daisy, Missouri Puzzle, Missouri Rose, Missouri Star, Missouri Sunflower, Missouri Wonder, Missouri Beauty, Missouri Trouble, Missouri Corn Field	Texas	Texas Tears, Texas Star, Texas Treasure, Texas Tulip, Texas Yellow Rose, Texas Cactus Basket, Texas Sunflower
		Utah	Utah Star
Montana	Montana Maze	Vermont	Vermont Maple Leaf
Nebraska	Nebraska Windmill	Virginia	Virginia Rose, Virginia Snowball, Virginia Star, Virginia Lily, Tree of Life
Nevada	Nevada		
New Hampshire	New Hampshire Granite Rock	Washington	Washington Evergreen, Washington Pavement, Washington Puzzle, Washington Star, Washington's Own, Washington Sidewalk
New Jersey	New Jersey		
New Mexico	New Mexican Star, Santa Fe Trail	West Virginia	West Virginia Lily, West Virginia Star
New York	New York Beauty, Albany	Wisconsin	Wisconsin Star, Wisconsin
North Carolina	North Carolina Lily, North Carolina Rose, North Carolina Star, North Carolina Beauty	Wyoming	Wyoming Valley

BIBLIOGRAPHY

Atkins, Jacqueline M. and Tepper, Phyllis A. *New York Beauties: Quilts from the Empire State*. New York: Dutton Studio Books in Association with the Museum of American Folk Art, 1992.

Brackman, Barbara. *An Encyclopedia of Pieced Quilt Patterns: Volume I*. Lawrence, KS: Barbara Brackman, 1979.

"Hawaii." *Quilter's Newsletter Magazine* (July/August 1989): 26-27.

"Kansas Patterns." *Quilter's Newsletter Magazine* (January 1987): 28-29, 62.

"Oregon and the Oregon Trail." *Quilter's Newsletter Magazine* (April 1991): 22-26, 62.

"Quilts on the Kansas Frontier." *Kansas History*, Vol. 13, No. I (Spring 1990): 13-23.

Bresenhan, Karoline Patterson and Puentes, Nancy O'Bryant. *Lone Stars: A Legacy of Texas Quilts, 1836-1936*. Austin: University of Texas Press, 1986.

Clark, Ricky, Knepper, George W., and Ronsheim, Ellice, *Quilts in Community: Ohio's Traditions*. Nashville: Rutledge Hill Press, 1991.

Clarke, Mary Washington. *Kentucky Quilts and Their Makers*. Lexington: The University of Kentucky Press, 1976.

Finley, John and Holstein, Jonathan. *Kentucky Quilts 1800-1900*. Louisville: The Kentucky Quilt Project, Inc., 1982.

Goldman, Marilyn and Wiebusch, Marguerite. *Quilts of Indiana: Crossroads of Memories*. Bloomington: Indiana University Press, 1991.

Granick, Eve Wheatcroft. *The Amish Quilt*. Intercourse, PA: Good Books, 1989.

Hoffman, Victoria. *Quilts: A Window To The Past*. North Andover, MA: Museum of American Textile History, 1991.

Homage to Amanda: Two Hundred Years of American Quilts. San Francisco: R K Press, 1984.

Horton, Laurel and Myers, Lynn Robertson. *Social Fabric: South Carolina's Traditional Quilts*, Columbia, SC: McKissick Museum, The University of South Carolina, 1985.

Khin, Yvonne M. *The Collector's Dictionary of Quilt Names & Patterns*. Washington, D.C,: Acropolis Books Ltd., 1980.

Lasansky, Jeannette. *In the Heart of Pennsylvania: 19th & 20th Century Quilt Making Traditions*. Lewisburg, PA: Oral Traditions Project of the Union County Historical Society, 1985.

Laury, Jean Ray. *Ho for California! Pioneer Women and Their Quilts*. New York: E.P. Dutton, 1990.

Orlofsky, Patsy and Orlofsky, Myron. *Quilts in America*. New York: McGraw-Hill Book Company, 1974.

Ramsey, Bets and Trechsel, Gail Andrews. *Southern Quilts: A New View*. Virginia: EPM Publications, 1991.

Ramsey, Bets and Waldvogel, Merikay. *The Quilts of Tennessee: Images of Domestic Life Prior to 1930*. Nashville: Rutledge Hill Press, 1986.

Sienkiewicz, Elly. *Baltimore Beauties and Beyond: Studies in Classical Album Quilt Applique: Volume Two*. Lafayette, CA: C & T Publishing, 1991.

Silber, Julie, Ferrero, Pat, and Hedges, Elaine. *Hearts and Hands: The Influence of Women & Quilts on American Society*. San Francisco: The Quilt Digest Press, 1987.

NOTES

1. Jacqueline M. Atkins and Phyllis A. Tepper, *New York Beauties. Quilts from the Empire State* (New York: Dutton Studio Books in Association with the Museum of American Folk Art, 1992) p. 101.

2. Elly Sienkiewicz, *Baltimore Beauties and Beyond: Studies in Classic Album Quilt Applique: Volume Two* (Lafayette, CA: C &T Publishing, 1991) p. l5.

3. Ibid.

4. Bets Ramsey and Gail Andrews Trechsel, *Southern Quilts: A New View* (Virginia: EPM Publications, 1991) p. 31.

5. Ibid, p. 35.

6. Ibid, p. 35.

7. John Finley and Jonathan Holstein, *Kentucky Quilts: 1800-1900* (Louisville, KY: The Kentucky Quilt Project, Inc., 1982) p. 35.

8. Ibid, p. 57.

9. Karoline Patterson Bresenhan and Nancy O'Bryant Puentes, *Lone Stars: A Legacy of Texas Quilts, 1836-1936* (Austin: University of Texas Press, 1986) p. l9.

10. Ibid, p. 15.

11. Ibid, p. l7.

12. Ricky Clark, George W. Knepper, and Ellice Ronsheim, *Quilts in Community: Ohio's Traditions* (Nashville: Rutledge Hill Press, 1991) p. 9.

13. Ibid, p. 81.

14. Eve Wheatcroft Granick, *The Amish Quilt* (Intercourse, PA: Good Books 1989) pp. 107-108.

15. Ibid, p. 116.

16. Jean Ray Laury, *Ho for California! Pioneer Women and Their Quilts* (New York: E.P. Dutton, 1990) p. 12.

17. Patsy and Myron Orlofsky, *Quilts in America* (New York: Abbeville Press, 1992) p. 276.

PHOTO CREDITS